Judaism: A Very Short Introduction

'This book will serve a very useful purpose indeed. I'll use it myself to discuss, to teach, argue with, and disagree with, in the Jewish manner!'
Rabbi Lionel Blue

'a magnificient achievement. Dr Solomon's treatment, fresh, very readable, witty and stimulating, will delight everyone interested in religion in the modern world.'
Louis Jacobs, University of Lancaster

'Throughout Norman Solomon's *Judaism* there is a freshness of approach which will make it interesting to those who already know something about Judaism. The conversational style will also make it variable for beginners.'
Marcus Braybrook, *Church Times*

VERY SHORT INTRODUCTIONS are for anyone wanting a stimulating and accessible way in to a new subject. They are written by experts, and have been published in more than 25 languages worldwide.

The series began in 1995, and now represents a wide variety of topics in history, philosophy, religion, science, and the humanities. Over the next few years it will grow to a library of around 200 volumes – a Very Short Introduction to everything from ancient Egypt and Indian philosophy to conceptual art and cosmology.

Very Short Introductions available now:

ANCIENT PHILOSOPHY
  Julia Annas
THE ANGLO-SAXON AGE
  John Blair
ANIMAL RIGHTS   David DeGrazia
ARCHAEOLOGY   Paul Bahn
ARCHITECTURE
  Andrew Ballantyne
ARISTOTLE   Jonathan Barnes
ART HISTORY   Dana Arnold
ART THEORY   Cynthia Freeland
THE HISTORY OF
  ASTRONOMY   Michael Hoskin
ATHEISM   Julian Baggini
AUGUSTINE   Henry Chadwick
BARTHES   Jonathan Culler
THE BIBLE   John Riches
BRITISH POLITICS
  Anthony Wright
BUDDHA   Michael Carrithers
BUDDHISM   Damien Keown
CAPITALISM   James Fulcher
THE CELTS   Barry Cunliffe
CHOICE THEORY
  Michael Allingham
CHRISTIAN ART   Beth Williamson
CLASSICS   Mary Beard and
  John Henderson
CLAUSEWITZ   Michael Howard
THE COLD WAR
  Robert McMahon

CONTINENTAL PHILOSOPHY
  Simon Critchley
COSMOLOGY   Peter Coles
CRYPTOGRAPHY
  Fred Piper and Sean Murphy
DADA AND SURREALISM
  David Hopkins
DARWIN   Jonathan Howard
DEMOCRACY   Bernard Crick
DESCARTES   Tom Sorell
DRUGS   Leslie Iversen
THE EARTH   Martin Redfern
EGYPTIAN MYTHOLOGY
  Geraldine Pinch
EIGHTEENTH-CENTURY
  BRITAIN   Paul Langford
THE ELEMENTS   Philip Ball
EMOTION   Dylan Evans
EMPIRE   Stephen Howe
ENGELS   Terrell Carver
ETHICS   Simon Blackburn
THE EUROPEAN UNION
  John Pinder
EVOLUTION
  Brian and Deborah Charlesworth
FASCISM   Kevin Passmore
THE FRENCH REVOLUTION
  William Doyle
FREUD   Anthony Storr
GALILEO   Stillman Drake
GANDHI   Bhikhu Parekh

Available soon:

For more information visit our web site

www.oup.co.uk/vsi

Norman Solomon

JUDAISM

A Very Short Introduction

OXFORD
UNIVERSITY PRESS

OXFORD
UNIVERSITY PRESS

Great Clarendon Street, Oxford OX2 6DP

Oxford University Press is a department of the University of Oxford.
It furthers the University's objective of excellence in research, scholarship,
and education by publishing worldwide in

Oxford New York

Auckland Bangkok Buenos Aires Cape Town Chennai
Dar es Salaam Delhi Hong Kong Istanbul Karachi Kolkata
Kuala Lumpur Madrid Melbourne Mexico City Mumbai Nairobi
São Paulo Shanghai Taipei Tokyo Toronto

Oxford is a registered trade mark of Oxford University Press
in the UK and in certain other countries

Published in the United States
by Oxford University Press Inc., New York

British Library Cataloguing in Publication Data

Data available

Library of Congress Cataloging in Publication Data

Data available

ISBN 978-0-19-285390-5

15 17 19 20 18 16 14

Typeset by RefineCatch Ltd, Bungay, Suffolk
Printed in Great Britain by
Ashford Colour Press Ltd, Gosport, Hampshire

Hath not a Jew eyes? Hath not a Jew hands, organs, dimensions, sense, affections, passions! Fed with the same food, hurt with the same weapons, subject to the same diseases, healed by the same means, warmed and cooled by the same winter and summer, as a Christian is? If you prick us do we not bleed?

William Shakespeare, *The Merchant of Venice*, III. i. 63

Contents

List of Illustrations

List of Tables

1. Jewish immigrants to Israel from various countries. Note the wide range of features indicating varied ethnic origins.

Introduction

Finding the right words

You are reading a book written in the English language. The English language is not neutral. It evolved in a Christian civilization; it comes ready loaded with a cargo of Christian concepts and assumptions. As Christianity was born out of a conflict within first-century Judaism, and defined itself as against Judaism, it is difficult from within a Christian culture and language to look at Judaism with the innocence you might look at, say, Shinto or Buddhism. Just think of some of the offensive overtones which have been carried in English by the simple word 'Jew'.

If you find yourself asking questions like, 'What do Jews believe about Jesus?', or 'What is more important in Judaism, faith or works?', you have got off on the wrong footing; you are approaching Judaism with cultural baggage imported from Christianity. You will find answers to some questions of this kind in this book, but they will not help you to comprehend Judaism *as Judaism understands itself*, from within; Judaism simply does not define itself around Jesus, nor does it assume that faith and works are opposing concepts.

So let us make a fresh start and try to discover what it's like to be a Jew, how Judaism looks *from within*. Here is a list of key terms drawn up by a class of Christian students who were trying to identify the terms that might be useful to explain to others what it was like to be a Christian:

- God the Father, Son, and Holy Spirit
- Resurrection
- salvation
- Baptism
- forgiveness
- Crucifixion
- conversion
- Confirmation
- Ascension
- justification
- Scriptures
- faith
- love
- Nativity
- Holy Communion
- prayer
- trust
- fellowship
- 'born again'
- obedience
- eternal life
- discipleship

The next list was drawn up by a religious Jew who wanted to explain his faith to a group of Christians:

- God (personal, historical, protean relationship)
- Torah (the way, instruction, teaching, *not* law)
- *mitzva* ('commandment' = the practical unit of Torah = good deed)
- *avera* (transgression, sin)
- Free Will
- *teshuva* (penitence, 'returning' to God)
- *tefilla* (prayer)
- *tsedaka* ('fairness', 'correctness' = charity)
- *hesed* (love, compassion, kindness)
- *yetser tov* ('good impulse' – the innate, psychological, tendency to do good), contrasted with *yetser hara* (the impulse to do evil; the cause and the remedy for unfaithfulness to God lie within the individual)
- Israel (people, land, covenant).

Some of the terms (God, Torah, Israel) are familiar enough to English-speaking Christians; but the compiler of the list evidently thought they should be glossed, because, despite the familiarity of the words, they might be misunderstood. Rather a lot of the words, however, are Hebrew; though they are everyday Hebrew words, 'easy' words in that language, it is very difficult to formulate their meaning in English.

As it happens, all of the words in the Christian list except the Christological group 'Son,' 'Crucifixion', 'Ascension', and 'Nativity' might well be used in a Jewish conversation. But they would carry different nuances, and a different 'weight' within the system. It is precisely words such as 'covenant', 'salvation', and 'scripture', widely used in both faith traditions, that cause the most confusion; their use overlaps, but does not entirely coincide. Sometimes, the two religions are divided rather than united by a common language.

Do not worry that the Hebrew words sound as if they might be hard to remember or to understand. They will be explained again whenever necessary, but the best way to pick them up is in context, in reading this book or others, or in your conversations with Jews who use them naturally. It is just like learning a language – in fact, it *is* learning a language, the 'natural' language of Judaism.

No religion is an abstraction. Its adherents may claim that God inspired it, or even that he dictated its texts, and that it is eternally valid. But the texts have to be interpreted by people and implemented in the lives of people, and the story which will unfold on the pages ahead is the story of how Jews have lived with their texts for the past two thousand years.

Our story has four *dramatis personae*: God, the Torah, the people of Israel, and the surrounding world. It is a story in which relationships are important, and the 'particular' (Israel) is in constant interaction with the 'universal' (humanity as a whole, in the shape of the surrounding culture). There are challenges and responses, tensions and resolutions, tragedies and joys.

'Judaism' is the religion of the Jews. Obvious. But who *are* the Jews? That will be the theme of Chapter 1. For the moment, we will regard as Jews all members of those groups today who define themselves as Jews in positive relation to the traditions formulated by the rabbis of the Talmud (you can find out about the Talmud in Chapter 3). This definition excludes 'the religion of the Old Testament', still presented as 'Judaism' in reactionary theological colleges. The world of the rabbis is grounded in that of the Hebrew scriptures on which it rests its authority, but as we shall see it is far from a literal reading of the text.

Likewise, the definition excludes other 'Jewish sects' which flourished in the first century – for instance, Essenes, Sadducees, Samaritans, and 'Jewish Christians', though we will meet some of these groups in Chapter 2, when we tell the story of how Judaism and Christianity, which were at first one religion, split apart.

We will focus on religion. Religion cannot be divorced from society or from history or from the emotional experiences and intellectual insights of its adherents. Therefore, some information about Jewish society and history will be included.

And we will make our own choice amongst the great schools of Jewish historiography, who tell the same story so differently from one another. There is, for instance, the 'lachrymose' school, to whom Jewish history is a vale of tears and suffering and martyrdom as one persecution followed another; this has been with us since Ephraim of Bonn, in the twelfth century, composed his famous martyrology in the wake of the massacres of Jews in the Rhineland, England, and France which accompanied the Second Crusade. Then there is the 'Jerusalem' school (Ben-Zion Dinur), in whose eyes all Jewish history relates to the Land of Israel, and at the opposite pole the great historian Simon Dubnow who stressed the positive achievement of 'Diaspora Judaism'. And there are the traditional theologians who, in true biblical style, see history as the narration of the people's sinfulness and penitence and God's punishment and reward, or who divide history into great 'pre-ordained' cycles, culminating with the arrival of the Messiah. Sherira Gaon, in tenth-century Babylonia, set the pattern for those to whom history meant tracing authentic tradition back to Moses. Franz Rosenzweig, in twentieth-century Germany, seems to deny that history is significant at all: 'We see God in each ethical action, but not in the finished whole, in history; for why would we need a God, if history were divine?'

For us, however, the emphasis will lie with the *creative* history of Judaism. The suffering and the persecutions and the forced migrations cannot be denied, but amazingly throughout the centuries the spirit has flourished with a still unending procession of poets and saints, of philosophers and of Bible commentators, of grammarians and talmudists, of lawyers and satirists and pastors and schoolmen, of unsung women and men of humble faith.

Chapter 1
Who are the Jews?

Is the tomato a fruit or a vegetable? To the botanist it is undoubtedly a fruit, to the chef a vegetable, but what would the tomato itself say? If it thought about the matter at all, it would probably have the same sort of identity crisis Jews are apt to get when people try to strait-jacket them as a race, an ethnic group, or a religion. Neither tomatoes nor Jews are particularly complicated or obscure when left to themselves, but they also don't fit neatly into the handy categories such as fruit or vegetable or nation or religion which are so useful for pigeonholing other foods and people.

How would you recognize a Jew if you bumped into him or her in the street? Since there are black as well as white Jews, oriental as well as occidental, converts as well as 'natives', atheist and agnostic as well as many types of religious Jews, is there any way to describe them collectively? How many of them are there? Where do they live?

Who the Jews used to be

The question of Jewish identity is surprisingly new. Nobody in medieval Christendom, for instance, thought there was a problem. They *knew* who the Jews were. The Jews were a 'special people', 'the chosen people', as it says in the Bible, chosen by God to be the vehicle of His revelation. But they had rejected Jesus, and therefore were accursed and condemned to lowly status until, in the fullness of time, they would recognize Jesus. By the late Middle Ages the Christian prophecy had fulfilled itself; Christians, by the exercise of political power, had actually brought the Jews to the lowly social state they had prophesied for them. Jews were confined to ghettos, made to wear distinctive clothing, excluded from guilds and professions and the ownership of land, vilified from the pulpit as killers of Christ, accused of poisoning wells (during the Black Death), of desecrating the Host, of murdering Christian children to use their blood for the Passover (the so-called 'Blood Libel'), and of almost every villainy that a warped mind could project on an alien group.

It is revealing, and rather shocking, to look at the way Jews have been portrayed in Christian religious art, especially in the west. Prior to the twelfth century they have no physical features to distinguish them from other people. Then, suddenly, there is a change, and Europe's Jews acquire hooked noses, webbed feet, and other aspects of what was thought to be the physiognomy of the devil; even in the twentieth century the folk belief persists in parts of Europe that Jews have horns. But, of course, it was not the Jews who mysteriously changed their appearance in the twelfth century and changed back again in the modern period, but Christian iconography, which articulated the myth of Jewish alliance with the devil.

The stereotypes generated within medieval 'Christendom' persisted even when the system collapsed under the impact of the Enlightenment. Even a champion of the Enlightenment such as Voltaire regarded the Jews as a reprobate and inferior race. In place of the theological anti-Judaism of the Church there came into being a racial 'anti-Semitism', which culminated in the Nazi *Endlösung*, or Final Solution, the project of humiliating and physically exterminating the 'Jewish race'.

The Nazis, however, had a problem. By 1933 it was transparently obvious that Jews did *not* have tails, horns, or any other gross features to distinguish them from other Germans (or Poles, or whatever). So, whilst Goebbels and his propaganda machine revived the medieval caricatures for publication in *Der Stürmer*, the reality of Jewish 'normality' was so far from the fantasy of Jewish racial distinctiveness that the Nuremberg laws had to define Jews lamely as anyone who had at least one Jewish great-grandparent – that is, 12½ per cent of 'Jewish blood'. Ominously, the Nazis based their early anti-Jewish laws – including boycott, segregation, and distinctive clothing – on those of Pope Innocent III's Fourth Lateran Council of 1215; a major aim of such legislation was to isolate Jews by making them *look* different from other people, despite the fact that nature had inconveniently fashioned them much the same as everyone else.

How Jews used to think of themselves

For as long as the surrounding cultures, Christian or Muslim, persisted in defining Jews as 'a people apart', and setting up laws to ensure this separateness, Jews internalized their social condition and themselves interpreted it in the old biblical terms. They saw themselves as God's chosen people, a nation in exile from its land. They agreed with their oppressors that they were exiled on account of their sins. However, the conclusions they based on this were different from those of the Christians and Muslims. Whereas Christians and (to a lesser extent) Muslims thought God's punishment of the Jews was a rejection and an abandonment, the Jews themselves understood it as a confirmation of their special 'chosen' status, for 'those whom He loves does the Lord chastise' (Prov. 3: 12). The nations amongst whom they were exiled were like the 'unclean' idolaters of old, whose blandishments and evil influence must at all costs be resisted, until such time as God in His infinite mercy chose to redeem and vindicate His people.

So throughout the Middle Ages, and much later wherever medieval attitudes and social structures persisted, Jews had no 'identity problem'. Their own traditions and the surrounding cultures reinforced one another in drawing sharp lines to set Jews apart from their geographical neighbours.

There was always, of course, a fuzzy margin, but it was a small one, easily decided by traditional rules. What, for instance, was the status of the child of Jewish parents who had, perhaps, been captured by an enemy, brought up as a Christian, and then returned to the Jewish fold? Or if (as may have happened not infrequently) a Jewish woman was raped by a Christian soldier or overlord, what was the status of her child? The rule, dating back at least to Roman times, was clear. The child of a Jewish mother was Jewish, and the child of a Jewish father by a non-Jewish woman was not Jewish unless and until formally converted. This is still the rule amongst most Jewish groups, though recently under the influence of the trend towards gender equality Reform Congregations in the USA have decided that, if either parent is Jewish, the child has full rights in the Jewish community without the need for formal conversion (see pages 104–5).

Who the Jews think they are now

In his work on Jewish identity Michael Meyer, who is professor of Jewish history at the Hebrew Union College Jewish Institute of Religion in Cincinnati, draws on the research of the sociologist Erik H. Erikson for his understanding of identity as

> those totalities of characteristics which individuals believe to constitute their selves. Individual identity is built upon pre-adult identifications with persons close to the child, with their values and behaviour patterns. As the individual becomes an adult these identifications must be integrated not only with one another but with the norms of the society in which the individual will play a role. This latter process represents 'identity formation' . . .

Integration 'with the norms of the society in which the individual will play a role' posed no great problem to the ghetto Jew; the norms and values of the limited society of which he felt himself a part – namely, Jewish society – did not conflict seriously with the norms and values he had acquired from the family that nurtured him. Family, community, and alienation from what lay beyond, combined to circumscribe a clear identity.

However, as Jews gradually gained civil rights in Europe and America and felt themselves citizens of the new nations, or even of the whole world, many of them were exposed to radically different norms and values from those of their childhood. Identity became less clear, less secure.

Meyer claims that three factors contributed to the formation of contemporary Jewish identity – namely, the Enlightenment, anti-Semitism, and the rise of the State of Israel. Let's see how these factors have operated.

The process of enlightenment through which Jews, as they were released from the restrictions of ghetto life, themselves became attuned to modern culture, meant that it became necessary to justify their behaviour by reason, the common basis of discourse, rather than by appeal to any authority, such as that of special Revelation. It also meant that public law should treat all people equally; this brought new civil rights to Jews, but at the same time denied their self-understanding as a 'special people'.

Perhaps no one put this more sharply than Count Clermont-Tonnerre, arguing before the National Assembly of the French Revolutionary government in 1789 for full citizenship of Jews: 'One must refuse everything to the Jews as a nation but one must give them everything as individuals; they must become citizens.' Jews, that is, were to be granted full rights as French citizens; but, in return, they had to abandon their collective distinctiveness and autonomy. Individual choice was to

2. Few leaders contributed more to implementing equal rights in Europe than Napoleon Bonaparte. In 1807 he convened a 'Sanhedrin' of Jewish notables to authorize the commitments he expected as a basis for full citizenship.

replace traditional communal authority, and religion would be a 'private' matter. Though many Jews welcomed this change, which quickly spread through Western and parts of Central Europe, some of the traditionalists opposed it vehemently, sensing a threat to established community authority and to traditional Jewish belief and practice. As Peter Berger has argued, heresy became the common condition in modernity once the plausibility structure of traditional beliefs was called into question and individual choice replaced the unquestioned acceptance of community authority.

Anti-Semitism, according to Meyer, has had an ambiguous effect on Jewish identity. On the one hand, rejection by the outside world has led to the reaffirmation of Jewish identity; movements of religious renewal have often flourished at times of discrimination or persecution, as enlightenment ideals of reason and universality have lost their attractiveness. The Damascus Affair of 1840, when the Jews of that city were accused of ritual murder and threatened with mass execution, stirred protest meetings amongst Jews as far away as the USA, provoked the intervention of Moses Montefiore of England and Adolphe Crémieux of France, and generally rallied Jews to an overall sense of purpose. The Mortara Affair of 1858, when a Jewish child was secretly baptized by a Christian domestic and abducted to a monastery, led directly to the formation in 1859 of the Board of Delegates of American Israelites and in 1860 of the French Alliance Israélite Universelle, which, like the Board of Deputies of British Jews set up in 1760 at the accession of George III, fostered a sense of Jewish solidarity whilst serving the primary cause of the defence of Jewish rights.

On the other hand, anti-Semitism has led Jews to turn away from identification with the Jewish community and to seek to lose or conceal their Jewish identity by merging with the surrounding culture; when Jews perceive that they are devalued by non-Jews, they may feel devalued in their own eyes, somehow internalizing the prejudice against them and falling prey to self-hatred. People change their names, appearance, or habits, to merge as far as possible with the surroundings, so that their Jewishness is not immediately apparent; in the words of Michael Meyer, 'antisemitic prejudice produces a heightened Jewish self-consciousness in the presence of gentiles, which results in the endeavor to keep Jewishness as invisible as possible for as long as possible to the eye of the untrustworthy outsider whose favour is sought'.

Karl Marx's early (1844) essay *On the Jewish Question* is a fascinating example of an intellectual form of Jewish self-hatred. He argues that Judaism is neither religion nor people-hood but the desire for gain; totally ignoring the vast Jewish proletariat of Central and Eastern Europe, he equates Jews, and the Christians whose religion derives from them, with the 'enemy' – namely, bourgeois capitalism. Clearly, he is fleeing his own Jewish identity (he was baptized at the age of 6, but was descended from rabbis on both sides of the family), 'assimilating' to the cultural milieu of the anti-Semitic Feuerbach, whose perverse definition of Judaism he has adopted, and finding refuge from Jewish particularism in socialist universalism.

Amongst Marx's close associates was Moses Hess, slightly older than Marx, and a notable socialist philosopher in his own right. In an essay written early in his career he expressed an attitude towards Judaism similar to that of Feuerbach and Marx. Later, he came to terms with his Jewish identity, which he reaffirmed not in religious terms but in national terms in his seminal work *Rome and Jerusalem*. Hess, that is, had responded to the third determinant of Jewish identity in modern times, the concept of the 'return to Zion'.

The paradox of Zionism (the term was coined only in 1892) lies in its twin origins, religious and secular. In the religious sense, the return to Zion is as old as God's promise to Abraham of the land in which he dwelled, and it has been reinforced throughout the ages through scripture, prayer, and the pious desire to fulfil God's commandments in the holy land. As early as 1782 Elijah of Vilna experienced a 'vision' calling for a return to Zion accompanied by a practical programme of regeneration of the land; whilst in the 1840s a Serbian rabbi, Yehuda Alkalai, undoubtedly influenced by Balkans nationalism, reformulated the ancient dream of the return to Zion in something approaching contemporary political terms.

The chief political thrust, however, came later in the century, from secular socialist Jews, such as Moses Hess, and eventually Theodor Herzl, the 'father of modern Zionism', all of whom rejected traditional religious beliefs. These men had discovered that enlightenment and universalism eroded Jewish identity but nevertheless failed to eliminate anti-Semitism. Their dissatisfaction with universalism echoed that of other nineteenth-century nationalist philosophers and politicians, but they found that it was impossible to commit themselves to local European nationalisms without abandoning their Jewishness. They solved the dilemma by cultivating a specifically Jewish nationalism – namely, Zionism.

Asher Ginzburg, better known by his Hebrew pseudonym Ahad Ha-Am ('one of the people'), consciously attempted to formulate a secular Jewish identity. His 'cultural Zionism' was a call to return to the physical land of Israel and to create there a new Jewish culture which, whilst preserving prophetic morality and Pharisaic balance of body and intellect, would be free of religious dogma and of the restrictions of rabbinic ritual.

The secularist attitude of the leading political Zionists was anathema to the religious leaders, many of whom opposed the movement even whilst nurturing their own dreams of a return to the land in the days of the Messiah. However, religious Zionist movements were eventually formed, and, especially since the Holocaust and the actual establish- ment of the Jewish state, religious Jews have emigrated to the State of Israel in substantial numbers and given it devoted support. The old conflicts between religious and secular Jews have by no means disappeared, however, but constantly resurface in political debate and social tensions within Israel itself.

Where are Jews to be found?

Before the outbreak of war in 1939 about ten million Jews lived in Europe, five million in the Americas (mainly North), 830,000 in Asia (including Palestine), 600,000 in Africa, and a handful in Oceania, perhaps eighteen million altogether.

Six million (the precise figure is debated) perished. The emigration of Jews from the Jewish cultural heartlands of central Europe, the annihilation of the majority of those who remained, the growth of Jewish settlement in Palestine/Israel, and the expulsion or flight of Jews from many Near Eastern and North African lands, radically altered the demography of the Jewish world. North America and Israel are now home to the main concentrations of Jews, the Jewish population of France has overtaken that of the UK as the largest in Europe outside Russia, and the once thriving communities in Muslim countries such as Egypt, Iran, and Iraq have all but vanished (see Table 1.1).

Contemporary identity

In 1992 a Symposium on Jewish Identities in the New Europe was convened in Oxford. The convenor, social anthropologist Dr Jonathan Webber, warned against simplistic attempts to reduce Jewish identity to superficial characteristics, for these can be misleading. For instance, strictly Orthodox Hasidic Jews may appear by some of their forms of dress to be particularly backward-looking; but they have thrived in the most modern of metropolises such as New York – one reason being that they have found excellent ways of adapting to the demands of participating in the economic structures of modern capitalism.

TABLE 1.1. Countries with populations of at least 10,000 Jews
Many of these figures, especially those for countries of the former Soviet Union, are unreliable

1000s		1000s	
Argentina	240	Lithuania	11
Australia	106	Mexico	48
Austria	12	Moldova	65
Belgium	30	Morocco	10
Belorus	10	Panama	10
Brazil	250	Romania	14
Canada	356	Russia	1000
Chile	25	South Africa	90
Czech Republic	10	Spain	12
Denmark	10	Sweden	18
France	600	Switzerland	18
Germany	67	Turkey	25
Holland	25	UK	300
Hungary	100	Ukraine	600
Iran	25	Uruguay	35
Israel	5619	USA	5950
Italy	35	Venezula	20
Latvia	17		

Webber is right to give his warning, but the situation is even more complicated than he suggests. The identity of the individual incorporates many elements, and the Jewish elements are never more than part of a whole. European Jews of today form the Jewish aspects of their identity out of a wide range of options, opened up by study of the sources as well as through contact with other Jews. To some extent the options they actually choose will be influenced by family, community, personal experiences, and the ambient culture. Prominent amongst the considerations affecting identity, once they have acquired the basic knowledge, will be the impact of the Shoah (the Holocaust) and the significance of the State of Israel.

Most of the countries in which Jews live today have broadly secular government and religiously plural societies. This environment creates an unprecedented opportunity for the development of identity, enabling individual Jews to resist authoritarian definitions of 'Jewishness', including those made by Jewish leaders.

Of course, communities and even larger structures must form, and will have 'boundaries' which demand at least a minimum definition of what may or may not be included. Such communities and organizations should seek the maximum latitude in mutual acceptance and recognition. Some will feel insecure if norms are ill-defined, but this is a lesser evil than stifling individual freedom and the holding back the evolution of Judaism.

No one can know what forms Jewish identity will take when the dust has settled on the New Europe and if and when lasting peace comes in Israel and the Middle East. New and distinctive forms of Judaism and Jewish identity will doubtless emerge. Fools may predict what these Judaisms will be; they may be proved wrong, but there is no great harm in that. Knaves, who seek power, will try to impose their own patterns on the future; they will probably fail, and will certainly do great damage in the attempt.

Chapter 2
How did Judaism and Christianity split up?

The story begins

When did Judaism begin? Is it really 'the oldest religion in the world'? Certainly not, if you believe what the experts tell us about the way human beings evolved. Ancient Stone Age people, tens of thousands of years ago, pretty certainly had religious beliefs and ceremonies, as we can tell from the pictures they painted in their caves and the way they buried their dead. Egypt and its temples and religion were already old when Moses was a youth in Pharaoh's palace.

But perhaps you prefer to believe just the simple text of the Bible. In that case, the answer depends on what you mean by 'Judaism'. Do you mean the religion of Abraham (about eighteen centuries BCE), who is claimed to be the ancestor of the Jewish people (and also, incidentally, of the Arabs)?

Or did Judaism start only when Moses received the Ten Commandments at Mount Sinai, some four or five hundred years after Abraham? Or later, when the Hebrew scriptures ('Old Testament') were completed?

There is a big problem with any of these answers. What we recognize nowadays as Judaism differs in many ways from the biblical religion. For instance, Jews don't believe literally in 'an eye for an eye'; and Jewish

How the years are reckoned

Traditional Jews trace history according to the Bible back to Adam and Eve. That gives a date of 3760 BCE for the creation of Adam, which is why the 'Jewish year', still used for religious purposes, is that many years ahead of CE (=AD). For instance, 1998 is AM 5758, and 2000 is AM 5760 (AM stands for *anno mundi*, or years of the world since Creation).

tradition strongly favours the idea of life after death even though there is nothing clear on the subject in the Hebrew scriptures. So to talk about the Jewish religion as we know it today being three or four thousand years old is quite wrong. The most we can say is that the 'roots' of the Jewish religion – the earliest parts of the Bible – are that old.

When we talk about 'Judaism' in this book we mean much more than those roots, though. We mean 'rabbinic Judaism', the way of life formulated by the rabbis from about the second century onwards, and rooted in the Bible. This 'rabbinic Judaism' is the foundation of all the forms of Judaism that exist today. True, Reform Jews attach far less weight to what the rabbis said than Orthodox Jews do (differences between Orthodox and Reform are described in Chapter 7). But for both Reform and Orthodox Jews rabbinic Judaism is the reference point for their own beliefs and practices.

Some people describe rabbinic Judaism as the religion of the 'dual Torah', for, as well as a written Torah (the Hebrew scriptures), it recognizes an 'oral Torah', or tradition, by which the written is interpreted and supplemented. (You may come across the terms 'written law' and 'oral law', but 'law' is not an accurate translation of 'Torah', which is more like 'way' or 'instruction'.)

Now Christians as well as Jews like to trace their spiritual descent back to Moses, Abraham, and Adam and Eve (with the minor difference that, when Bishop Ussher calculated the creation of Adam and Eve, he made it 4004 BC rather than the Jewish 3760 BC). They claim the Torah – the Hebrew scriptures – as their own. Like Jews, they do not take the Hebrew scriptures in their plain sense. However, they interpret them not in accordance with the 'oral Torah' of the rabbis, but in the light of the New Testament.

But this difference in interpretation did not become clear until the letters of Paul were written. Up to a certain point in time, perhaps in the middle of the first century – the generation after Jesus – there was no dividing line between Judaism and Christianity. Jesus, indeed, never thought of himself as preaching a religion other than Judaism, or Torah; 'Do not think I have come to abolish the Law or the Prophets; I have come not to abolish but to fulfil' (Matt. 5: 17). If you had asked Jesus or any or his disciples what religion they were, they would have replied 'Jewish'.

So why did the two split apart and become two separate, if intimately related, religions? There is a traditional Jewish story about this, and a traditional Christian story.

Traditional Jewish story: Judaism is an ancient religion, received by Moses at Mount Sinai and preserved by the Jewish people unchanged ever since. At some time in the first century, Jesus followed by Paul set up a new religion, borrowing important bits from Judaism, abandoning the commandments, and mixing in some strange and incorrect ideas such as the notion that Jesus was the Messiah or even the 'incarnation' of God.

Traditional Christian story: Judaism is an ancient religion, received by Moses at Mount Sinai and carefully preserved by the Jews ever since. At some time in the first century, Jesus came and 'perfected' this religion, bringing it to its fulfilment. Unfortunately the Jews did not appreciate what had happened, and stubbornly continued with the obsolete form of the religion.

What both versions of the story have in common is that there are two distinct religions, each of which descended fully-fledged from the sky (or was invented) at a particular point in time, the one in the days of Moses, the other in the days of Jesus. Where they differ is in their evaluation of the second event and its relationship with the first. But they agree that Judaism is the 'mother' religion, and Christianity the 'daughter', if (in the Jewish view) an errant one.

The news from the world of scholarship is that both versions are wide of the mark. Judaism did not spring into life fully mature one day around 1400 BCE, nor did Jesus in about the year 30 CE or even Paul a generation later proclaim a Christian creed or catechism like those of the mature Church. Both religions underwent centuries of development before their texts, practices, and beliefs attained their 'traditional' forms. They have coexisted and developed in response to changing circumstances and insights until the present day. Indeed, both Judaism and Christianity are even today reformulating themselves as vigorously as ever in the light of modern knowledge, evolving moral attitudes, and new understanding of the world's problems.

Strange as it may seem, the Talmud and other founding texts of rabbinic Judaism were actually written *later* than the Gospels, which were the founding texts of Christianity. When the Pope recently referred to Jews as the 'elder brother' of Christians he got it wrong; we are both, of course, 'children' of the Hebrew scriptures, but in terms of our defining texts (New Testament, or Talmud) it is Christians who are the 'elder brother'.

Where did Judaism and Christianity come from?

When you visit Israel today you can tour synagogues and churches, as well as Muslim, Druze, Bahai, and other holy places, and savour the range of forms of worship with which the country abounds. If you have a deeper thirst for knowledge and spiritual growth, you can study for a period at one or more of the numerous *yeshivot* or religious seminaries of the different religions and denominations, or sit at the feet of some great teacher who inspires you.

You could have done much the same in the days of Jesus. Many people did. Joseph the son of Mattathias, better known to posterity as the soldier and historian Flavius Josephus, undertook just such a tour as part of his personal spiritual quest as a teenager in the 50s of the first century. Later in life, when he lived in Rome under patronage of the emperor, he recorded his experiences in his autobiography and in his great work on *The Antiquities of the Jews*.

According to Josephus, Jews in the first century were divided into four sects, or 'philosophies'. The Pharisees – the group with whom he associated most strongly – live modestly, he says, in accordance with reason. They respect the elderly, and believe in divine providence, freedom of the will, and personal immortality; they are held in esteem by the people, who are guided by them in prayer and sacrifice. The Sadducees deny life after death, following only the explicit provisions of scripture. The Essenes – many scholars identify them as a sect now known through the Dead Sea Scrolls – ascribe all things to God, and teach the immortality of the soul. They are distinguished by their virtuous mode of life, restrained by excessive purity from sacrificing in the Temple, and share their property in common; they neither marry, nor keep servants. Josephus claims to have spent three years under one of their teachers, Banus, who 'lived in the desert, wore no other clothing than grew upon trees, and had no other food than what grew of its own accord'. The fourth group, with whom Josephus did not associate, he calls the Zealots; they agree in most things with the Pharisees but exceed them in their readiness to die for freedom from all rule save that of God.

Religious life in first-century Palestine was even more varied than Josephus suggests. There were no Muslim, Druze, or Bahai, as you will find in modern Israel. But there were the Samaritans, a Jewish sect with a distinct ethnic identity and a Temple of their own at Mount Gerizim. And there were mystics who claimed esoteric knowledge of the 'heavenly palaces' and the way of ascent to God. There were apocalyptic visionaries, who proclaimed God's judgement and the end of the world. By the time young Josephus embarked on his spiritual journey there must also have been some groups of followers of Jesus, though they don't seem to have attracted his attention. And, in addition to the varieties of Judaism, there were the pagan and 'mystery' cults which were wide-spread in the Roman Empire, and the Zoroastrian religion which was dominant in the East. Josephus shows little interest in these, but was evidently well versed in the Greek culture of his time, especially in history and philosophy.

So in the year 50 Christianity was a minor Jewish sect, and Judaism itself a minority cult within the Roman Empire. With the hindsight of history we know that the little Jesus groups would part from their 'parent' and within a few centuries replace the old pagan cults as the dominant religion of Europe, that the Pharisee 'philosophy' would evolve into rabbinic Judaism, and that, from the seventh century, Islam would carry similar ideas about God and society to much of Africa and Asia.

But just *why* did the followers of Jesus eventually separate themselves from their Jewish brethren? And why did such mutual hatred arise between two religions both of which preached love of one's neighbour?

Why did they split up?

The New Testament Book of The Acts of the Apostles, in chapter 15, has preserved an account of an extraordinary confrontation which took place amongst the leaders of the recently formed Christian sect, probably some time between 50 and 60 CE. By this time Paul, who had previously campaigned vigorously against the followers of Jesus, had experienced his famous vision on the road to Damascus and joined the sect he had previously despised. Together with his friend Barnabas, he returned from Antioch in Syria to canvass support from the Jerusalem leadership for his view that Gentile converts to Christianity need not be circumcised or obey 'the law of Moses'.

The debate was heated. Whilst Paul and Peter (both themselves Jews) argued that relaxing the strict requirements of the law would make it easier for Gentiles to convert, others present felt that full commitment to the Torah and its laws was vital. Eventually James, Jesus' brother, proposed that the burden should not be made too hard, but that Gentiles should at least be required to 'abstain from food polluted by idols, from sexual immorality, from the meat of strangled animals, and from blood' (Acts 15: 20); this compromise, the book relates, was adopted by the gathering, and a letter to that effect dispatched to Antioch, Syria, and Cilicia.

But we know from elsewhere that the compromise was not endorsed by all parties. On the one hand, Paul himself repeatedly declared the 'law of Moses' (of which the strangled meat and other prohibitions are part) as obsolete; on the other hand, the 'Jewish Christians', who observed fully the 'Torah of Moses', and who probably included James in their number, flourished for some time and, despite marginalization by Pauline Christians, continued in their distinct identity for centuries. We can only speculate as to their version of the Jerusalem meeting, for it was the followers of Paul who wrote the New Testament and so shaped later Christianity. History is written by the victors, and in such a way as to justify their interpretation of events.

Whatever the truth about the meeting in Jerusalem, the account in the Acts highlights some of the factors which sundered apart Jews and Christians. Obviously, there was disagreement about whether certain laws of the Torah were still applicable. This was not just a quarrel about doctrine, but a serious social rift. A nation, or a religious community, expresses its identity through its laws, customs, and rituals. Minor disagreements or individual lapses can sometimes be contained, but a collective abandonment of the laws is likely to be perceived as a rejection of identity. Paul's plan to absorb Gentiles into the community of believers – to 'graft the wild olive' on to the root of the nourishing tree, as he put it (Rom. 11: 17) – proved incompatible with the way that Jews understood themselves as a people or a community. Instead of uniting 'Jew and Gentile', it generated two conflicting groups each of which claimed to be the 'true Israel'.

It is also clear from Acts that by the year 50 the followers of Jesus had constituted themselves into a distinctive group which opposed and were opposed by the Jewish religious leadership in Jerusalem. Other 'opposition' groups – the Dead Sea sects, for instance – fell out with the Jerusalem leadership without becoming a new religion. Why was this one different?

The claim that Jesus was the promised Messiah is not in itself enough to explain the rift; such claims had been made on behalf of others without such far-reaching consequences. Still, there was something unusual in a group proclaiming as Messiah someone known to be dead, and something paradoxical in making the claim that the Messiah had come when it was obvious to everyone that the yoke of Rome lay heavier than ever on the people and that the promised era of peace was not in sight.

Not one cause alone, but a unique combination of doctrinal differences, social factors, and external events, set Christianity on its course as a religion distinct from Judaism though closely related to it. The destruction of the Jerusalem Temple by the Romans in 70 hardened the division. Christians interpreted this event as God's rejection of the Jews and the confirmation of their own views. Jews interpreted it as just punishment for their sins but not rejection; it was like a father chastising his children. On a more down-to-earth level, when, following the sack of Jerusalem, the Emperor Vespasian imposed a *fiscus Judaicus* – a special tax on all Jews – there was strong material motivation to demonstrate distance from Judaism and allegiance to Rome.

Certainly, after 70 there was no going back. Doctrines hardened on both sides as Christians and Jews defined themselves in opposition to one another, and Christians developed the 'teaching of contempt' about Jews that was to cause so much misery and bloodshed until, detached from its Christian setting, it culminated in the Holocaust.

How did they both define themselves?

After 70 both Jews and Christians got on with the great work of self-definition. What did they believe about this world and the next? How should their communities be set up? What forms of prayer and what special days and what ceremonies should they adopt?

Because Jesus Christ was so central for them, Christians expended much energy in defining belief. The concept of the Trinity was constantly debated, and those who disagreed with the prevailing view were often vilified as heretics and persecuted. Since Jews rejected Christian claims for Jesus, they came in for special obloquy as 'enemies of Christ'. Judaism was castigated as an obsolete and discredited religion. The Fathers of the Christian Church, for all their preaching of love, openly expressed a hatred of Jews and Judaism which added a cosmic dimension to the anti-Semitism occasionally found in pagan classical authors; the Jews had 'killed Christ'.

3. Symbolic statues of the Church and the Synagogue, at the Liebfrauenkirche, Trier, Germany. The Church stands proud and upright; the Synagogue stands blindfold, humble, crown falling from her head, sceptre broken, and the Tablets of Stone upside down.

Divided by a Common Scripture

The Church father Origen, who died in 254, lived in Caesarea, Palestine; amongst his Jewish contemporaries was Rabbi Yohanan of Tiberias. Both commented on the biblical Song of Songs; both interpreted it as allegory. For Origen, it stands for God, or Christ, and his 'bride', the Church; for Yohanan, it is an allegory of the love between God and his people Israel.

An American scholar, Reuben Kimelman, has analysed their comments and found five consistent differences between them, corresponding to five major issues which divided Christians and Jews:

1. Origen writes of a Covenant *mediated* by Moses between God and Israel; that is, an *indirect* contact between the two, contrasted with the *direct* presence of Christ. Yohanan, on the other hand, refers to the Covenant as *negotiated* by Moses, hence received by Israel *direct* from God, as 'the kisses of his mouth' (S. of S. 1: 2). Yohanan emphasizes the closeness and love between God and Israel, whereas Origen sets a distance between them.

2. According to Origen the Hebrew scripture was 'completed', or 'superseded', by the New Testament. According to Yohanan scripture is 'completed' by the 'oral Torah', the interpretative tradition of the rabbis.

3. To Origen, Christ is the central figure, replacing Abraham, and completing the reversal of Adam's sin. To Yohanan, Abraham remains in place, and Torah is the 'antidote' to sin.

4. To Origen, Jerusalem is a symbol, a 'heavenly city'. To Yohanan, the earthly Jerusalem retains its status as the link between heaven and earth, the place where God's presence will again be manifest.

> **5.** Origen sees the sufferings of Israel as the proof of its repudiation by God; Yohanan accepts the suffering as the loving chastisement and discipline of a forgiving father.

The rabbis were less concerned with the precise definition of correct belief. Taking as axiomatic belief in God, his Revelation through Torah, and his 'election' (choice) of Israel, they defined Judaism in terms of the *mitzvot*, or divine commandments, ranging from 'love your neighbour as yourself' (Lev. 19: 18) and 'love the Lord your God' (Deut. 6: 5) to minutiae of religious ritual.

The Jewish sources are reticent about Christianity. On the whole, the rabbis tended to act as if Christianity did not exist, and simply to get on with the job of expounding the Torah and its laws. You have to read between the lines of their writings to discover whether they are making any response at all to Christian claims.

No one is sure to what extent Jewish and Christian teachers in the early centuries had meaningful direct contact with one another, or first-hand knowledge of each other's writings. The Christian Justin Martyr, active in Rome from about 140 to 170, composed a *Dialogue with Trypho* which purports to be the record of a dispute with a Jewish sage, but, despite the efforts of scholars, it is hard to equate Trypho's views with those of known Jewish sources.

There must have been contacts, for instance, in Caesarea, Palestine, in the third century, where there were both Jewish and Christian communities (see Box), or in Antioch, Syria, where St John Chrysostom preached his anti-Jewish diatribes in the following century, perhaps because he feared Christians were being attracted to the Synagogue. And, of course, there were individuals who 'changed sides' in one direction or another, and women who mediated ideas but whose contribution was not recorded.

It would be unfair to judge early Christianity and Judaism by their attitudes to one another, for in neither case was this at the top of their agenda. Yet the heritage of mistrust and mutual animosity still burdens us, and it is only in recent times that Christians have begun to come to terms with this dark side of their faith and the misery and suffering it has caused. Particularly since the Holocaust, though the foundations were laid earlier, Christian–Jewish dialogue has opened up avenues of reconciliation and led to revision of traditional Christian attitudes and theology with regard to Jews and Judaism.

Chapter 3
How did Judaism develop?

On 24 June 1985 the Vatican Commission for Religious Relations with the Jews issued a document with the unmemorable title 'Notes on the correct way to present the Jews and Judaism in preaching and catechesis in the Roman Catholic Church'. It contained these memorable words: 'We must remind ourselves how the permanence of Israel is accompanied by a continuous spiritual fecundity, in the rabbinical period, in the Middle Ages and in modern times, taking its start from a patrimony which we long shared', to which it added Pope John Paul II's observation that 'the faith and religious life of the Jewish people as they are professed and practised still today, can greatly help us to understand better certain aspects of the life of the Church'.

At last, after nineteen centuries, the truth has been allowed to surface. It is not only the Church which has suppressed it; the 'continuous spiritual fecundity' has too often been obscured by Jewish historians, who have been so concerned to demonstrate the sufferings and the martyrdoms of the Jewish people that they have allowed the record of persecution to overshadow the other side of the story, the spiritual and intellectual creativity of the Jews 'in the rabbinical period, in the Middle Ages and in modern times'.

It is remarkable that a people subjected to harassment, persecution and exile, and frequently deprived of normal means of livelihood and denied access to the great foundations of learning, should have produced a culture of such great vitality. The nine men and two women whose stories follow each illustrate some spiritual, intellectual or social value in Jewish life. Others might have been chosen – Gamaliel II, for instance, architect of the liturgy, or Yehuda Halevi, sublime poet and philosopher, or Glückel of Hamlin, whose Yiddish diary reveals the intimate spiritual concerns of a seventeenth-century mother. Or a hundred others. Any choice would be arbitrary.

Judah ha-Nasi – scholar, saint, leader

If anyone epitomizes rabbinic Judaism at the time of its formation, it is Judah, the Nasi ('prince') or Patriarch of the Jewish community round about the year 200. So great was the regard in which he was held by his disciples that they refer to him simply as 'rabbi' ('teacher'), or 'our holy rabbi', without any name being used; holiness, humility, and the fear of sin are the values with which he is associated. 'At Rabbi's death, humility and the fear of sin ceased', was the lament of his disciple Hiyya.

He was no cloistered saint, but an outstanding religious and political leader. He lived through much of his life in Galilee, and founded academies there at Bet Shearim and Sepphoris; visitors to Israel may still see remains of the synagogues in those towns with their partly preserved mosaics, as well as graves said to be those of Rabbi and his colleagues.

The decades before his birth had been disastrous for Judea. In 70, the Romans had crushed the First Revolt and destroyed the Jerusalem Temple; in 135, approximately the year of Judah's birth, the Emperor Hadrian had finally crushed the Second (Bar Kochba) Revolt, with huge loss of life and subsequent persecutions.

But by the time Judah rose to be Patriarch of Judea, under the reign of the Antonine emperor Marcus Aurelius, relations with Rome had eased.

Judah, a man of peace, and evidently at home in Roman culture, did what he could to consolidate relations with the occupying power. The Talmud records many anecdotes of the cordial relations between 'Rabbi and Antoninus'; there could be some historical foundation for such meetings in the visits to Palestine of the emperors Marcus Aurelius in 175 and Septimius Severus in 200.

In fact, the legendary 'conversations of Rabbi and Antoninus' suggest rather more than a superficial relationship. The Stoic philosophy to which Marcus Aurelius was devoted left its mark on Jewish as well as Christian ethics. Moreover, it is surely no coincidence that Rabbi's great undertaking, the creation of a comprehensive Jewish Code of Law, was formulated at the time when Gaius and Ulpian were laying foundations for the systematization of Roman Law.

The Code created under Rabbi's direction was called the Mishna ('teaching', or 'repetition'), and complements scripture as the foundation document of rabbinic Judaism. Its six volumes, the earliest systematic statement of Judaism, are far more than a legal code, for they encompass values as well as laws, ethical principles as well as rules, and are concerned with worship and purity as much as with civil and criminal jurisdiction and personal status. They were quickly accepted as authoritative and formed the basis on which the Talmud was developed (see Table 3.1).

Numerous tales are related of the personal life of Rabbi. One of the best known tells of his concern for animals. A calf was about to be slaughtered. It ran to Rabbi, nestled its head in his robe and whimpered. He said to it, 'Go! This is what you were created for!' As he did not show it mercy, heaven decreed suffering upon him. One day Rabbi's housekeeper was sweeping. She came across some young weasels and threw them and swept them out; he said, 'Let them alone! Is it not written, "His mercies extend to all His creatures" ' (Ps. 145: 9)? Heaven decreed, 'Since he is merciful, let us show him mercy'.

TABLE 3.1. The six orders of the Mishna

1. Seeds	Blessings and prayers
	Agricultural laws, such as the tithes and the sabbatical year
2. Appointed times	Sabbath and festivals
3. Women	Marriage and divorce; vows
4. Damages	Civil law
	The constitution of courts
	Legal procedure
	Ethics of the Fathers
5. Holy things	Temple sacrifices
	Permitted and forbidden foods
6. Purities	Purification through washing and bathing
	Degrees of ritual purity
	Things defined as 'unclean'

Stamaim – the nameless ones

(This is pronounced like 'stammer' + 'im', with the accent on 'im', the Hebrew masculine plural ending.) Stamaim is not the name of some saintly individual who became the subject of story and legend. It is not the name of anyone at all. It means 'the anonymous men', and scholars now use the term to refer to a group of men (although we do not know who they were, we are fairly certain that there were no women amongst them) who lived in Babylonia round about the sixth century and edited the text of the Talmud.

But we jump ahead of our story, for before the Stamaim there were three other groups, all ending with 'im' (accent on the last syllable), whose names we *do* know. The Tannaim were the rabbis whose names occur in the Mishna, right up to Judah the Patriarch himself, and their contemporaries. They were followed by the Amoraim, who discussed

Talmud = Mishna + Gemara

There are two Talmudim:

• The Talmud of the Land of Israel (also known as the Palestinian Talmud, or Yerushalmi, i.e. Talmud of Jerusalem), completed about 450 CE

• The Babylonian Talmud, completed about 550 CE. This is larger than the Yerushalmi, and considered to have greater authority.

their views, harmonizing apparent contradictions, deciding conflicts, extending the law, and applying it in new circumstances. Then came the Seboraim, who asked a lot of 'why' and 'what is the underlying concept' questions about the opinions of their predecessors – questions designed to understand rather than to challenge them, for so great was their respect for the earlier rabbis that they did not dare disagree with their rulings. The discussions of the Amoraim and Seboraim were recorded, selected, and edited in the Talmud, later known as Gemara (= 'learning', 'completion'), a vast Aramaic text which takes the form of a commentary on the Mishna.

The term 'Talmud' is now often used for Mishna and Gemara together. The Talmud really is the heart of Judaism. After the Bible, it is the book most studied by Jews, and the Bible itself is read in its light. But for all its importance, and despite the fact that it contains many hundreds of names (of Tannaim, Amoraim, and Seboraim), we do not know who actually put it all together and edited it. These editors told anecdotes, they made decisions, they knew how to present abstruse legal arguments in dramatic literary structures that would hold the students' attention; they collected tales and observations that would capture the imagination, often scaling the heights of moral and spiritual discernment, though occasionally betraying the prejudices of their age;

but they did not sign their names on any document. Probably they thought they were merely reproducing the words of the great masters of previous generations, and would have been genuinely shocked at the notion that they were themselves contributing anything original.

Every generation has its Stamaim, the anonymous scholars and humble practitioners who actually shape and implement the untidy inspirations of the wise 'named ones' who came before them.

Kahina Dahiya bint Thabbita ibn Tifan – warrior

Before the meteoric spread of Islam outwards from the Arabian peninsula towards the end of the seventh century many of the tribes of North Africa had been converted to Judaism or Christianity. Some no doubt accepted Islam willingly, but others opposed the conquering Arab armies and their new religion.

In what is now south-east Algeria was a powerful Berber tribe, the Jerawa, which had become Jewish. With Kahina at their head the Jerawa defeated the Arab army of Hasan ibn al Nu´man, holding up the Arab invasion of Africa and preventing its further progress into Spain. Kahina, however, was betrayed, and killed in battle around the year 700.

What sort of Judaism this fearsome Berber princess might have practised, and indeed whether she was in fact Jewish, it is impossible to say with certainty. But her story, which is repeated with embellishments by several Arab chroniclers, raises one of the big 'what if's' of history. What if she had consolidated her victory over Hasan and marched either back across North Africa towards Arabia or northwards into Spain? Would Europe and the Near East nevertheless have been divided into rival Christian and Muslim empires, or would our history have been radically different?

Whatever might have been, the reality which came about partly through Kahina's defeat was that of two constantly warring 'big powers', with Jews reduced to subservience throughout their domains.

Saadia Gaon (882–942) – philosopher

In 635 insurgent Arab tribes destroyed the Sassanid Empire in what is now Iraq, bringing with them the new religion of Islam. By this time the Babylonian Talmud was complete, and its contents were studied at the great academies of Sura and Pumbedita by the Euphrates. Each of these rival academies, the Oxford and Cambridge of Jewish Babylonia, had at its head a rabbi known by the title 'Gaon' ('illustrious'), whose responsibilities included administration of the law as well as spiritual direction and teaching. The lay head of this self-governing community was the Resh Galuta, or 'Head of the Exile', who claimed descent from king David and handled relations between the Jews and the Caliphate.

Jewish life flourished, at least intermittently, under the Abbasid caliphs of Baghdad (750–1258), and the Geonim (note once again the Hebrew masculine plural 'im') were called upon to answer queries from all parts of the Jewish world from Provence to Yemen. Frequently their replies were copied and preserved; in accordance with Jewish custom, such correspondence was eventually thrown away into a 'geniza' (pronounce 'g'neezah'), or repository for holy writings. Much of the contents of the Cairo geniza were brought about a century ago to the University Library at Cambridge, England; do not miss the opportunity to see an exhibition there or to hear a talk about this extraordinary collection.

Saadia ben Joseph was born in the village of Dilaz in the Fayyum (which is why he is known as al-Fayyumi) in Upper Egypt. He left Egypt in about 905 and for several years wandered between Palestine, Aleppo (Syria), and Baghdad. In 928, despite his foreign origin, he was appointed Gaon of the academy of Sura. He achieved note as philosopher, scientist, Talmudist, author, commentator, grammarian, translator, educator, and religious leader, but not without controversy in virtually every field.

Saadia wrote his great philosophical classic, *The Book of Doctrines and Beliefs*, during the years he was suspended from office and placed under arrest by David ben Zaccai, the 'Head of the Exile', because he refused ben Zaccai's order to sign a document he considered unjust. Saadia, who was well versed in Islamic *kalam* (theology) and *falasifa* (Aristotelian philosophy), believed in the supremacy of reason, including the moral sense. He held that God's ways and his revelation accord with reason not because God *defines* reason and justice; rather, God, in total freedom, acts and reveals himself in accordance with absolute standards of reason and justice. To put it another way, God does what is rational or just because it is a priori rational or just; it is not rational or just *because* God does it.

Saadia's epistemology derives from his emphasis on the supremacy of reason. All knowledge comes to us through sense experience, logical inference from sense experience, or an innate moral sense which is itself a form of 'rationality'. How do we know, for instance, that someone who claims God sent him to tell us to steal or fornicate, or that the Torah is no longer applicable, and bolsters his claim to prophecy by apparently performing miracles, is not to be believed? It is because reason tells us to act morally and that truth is preferable to falsehood.

The Torah itself conforms entirely with reason. Saadia divides the commandments into 'rational' and 'heard' – that is, those known by reason and those known primarily through revelation. Even though not all the commandments have obvious reasons, we can make an 'educated guess' at the reasons for the more obscure ones. But if the Torah conforms entirely with reason, why did God send messengers (prophets) to give it to us? Revelation was a special act of God's compassion, so that knowledge of Torah should be clear and available to all, even those who lacked philosophical ability or time to discover it for themselves.

Saadia was acquainted with the writings of other sects and religions. His refutations of Karaism (a Jewish sect which rejects the rabbinic tradition), as well as of Islam, Christianity, and 'dualist' religion, are well informed and based on rational arguments.

What's in a name?

Many famous people are known in Hebrew not by their actual name but by an abbreviation made from the initial consonants of their title and name.

So, Rabbi Shlomo Itzchaki (Solomon son of Isaac) is known as Rashi; Rabbi Moses ben Maimon (Maimonides) is known as Rambam.

Though he edited the Hebrew prayer book and composed some Hebrew liturgical poems, he wrote mostly in Arabic. An outstanding biblical scholar, he wrote numerous commentaries, and produced an Arabic translation of scripture used to this day.

Rashi (1040–1105) – commentator

Today, at Worms, in western Germany on the banks of the Rhine, you can visit Rashi's synagogue (reconstructed after having been demolished by the Nazis), see his chair, and explore a whole museum dedicated to him. You begin to feel his benign, fatherly presence, guiding you. It is a feeling familiar to generations of Jews who now, as ever, are introduced to both scripture and Talmud through his commentaries. He is *the* commentator, *par excellence*, on the Talmud. His gift of anticipating the reader's questions and of brief, clear explanation, make you feel that he is in the room with you, expounding the text, guarding you firmly but gently from error.

Most children get to know him – and the Bible and the Hebrew language – through his ever-popular Hebrew commentary on the Five Books of Moses. The enduring appeal perhaps comes from the inimitable style in which he presents homilies, legends, and explanations of the commandments, selected from Talmud and Midrash. Yet to scholars Rashi appears as a master of biblical language, who drew upon the work of generations of grammarians and lexicographers who had preceded him to make a clear distinction between what the Bible actually said (the *peshat*, or 'plain meaning'), and what was read into it *(derash*, homiletics) by tradition. Part of the homeliness, the sense of an actual teacher being present, when one reads Rashi, is the way he translates difficult terms into Old French, so that one can almost hear him talking to those around him.

The Commentary on the Pentateuch was the first dated printed Hebrew book (Reggio 1475), and has elicited more than 200 supercommentaries. It was often translated into Latin. Rashi's Bible commentaries exerted great influence on Nicholas de Lyra, and through him on Luther and other Christian Hebraists and the Reformation.

Rashi may have studied at Worms, but his home was Troyes, the capital of Champagne (now north-eastern France). He did not support himself as a rabbi, but cultivated vineyards; had he thought of putting bubbles in his wine, he would have been the first ever producer of authentic champagne!

Details of his life are sparse. He had three daughters, two of whom, Miriam and Yocheved, married his pupils; the name of the third is unknown. In about 1070 he founded a school which attracted many disciples, and which in the course of time and under the guidance of his sons-in-law and grandsons became the leading Ashkenazi academy of Torah.

His last years were saddened by the First Crusade (1095/6), in which he lost relatives and friends. The Selihot (penitential poems) he composed then manifest a spirit of sadness and the tender love of God; some of them remain in the liturgy.

Legends – about his descent from King David, his extensive travels, his meeting with Maimonides (who was not born until 1138!) – make up for the lack of verifiable facts. One legend says that his father cast into the sea a valuable gem coveted by Christians as an ornament for a religious statue, whereupon a mysterious voice announced he would have a learned son. Another tells how his mother was imperilled in a narrow street in Worms during her pregnancy, and a niche (still pointed out to tourists) miraculously opened to secrete her in a wall. Yet another relates that he foretold to Godfrey de Bouillon that the latter, setting off for the Crusade, would reign over Jerusalem for three days then be defeated and return home with three horses.

Abraham Ibn Ezra (1089–1164) – poet

Born in Toledo, Ibn Ezra achieved distinction as poet, grammarian, physician, philosopher, astrologer, and bible commentator. Of a critical turn of mind, he let drop a hint that there might be some doubt as to the Mosaic authorship of the Pentateuch; the hint was picked up six centuries later by Spinoza and led to modern Bible criticism. Though a confirmed astrologer, he was one of the few of his time who rejected belief in demons.

Ibn Ezra left Spain in 1140 and travelled through Italy, North Africa, and the Near East, and to Western Europe including France and England. In London he composed his main philosophical work, *Foundation of the Fear of God*, in which he expounds the Neoplatonic philosophy which features prominently in his biblical commentaries. The succinct and combative style of the commentaries won them lasting popularity; their influence on Christian Hebraism at the Renaissance was second only to that of Rashi.

Ibn Ezra won the friendship and esteem of scholars, but regarded his personal life ruefully, whether because of his 'exile' from Spain, or because of the loss of four of his children and the temporary conversion of the surviving son to Islam. He had a wry sense of humour; in an epigrammatic poem he laments:

> The sphere and the fixed constellations
> Strayed in their paths when I was born;
> If candles were my business
> The sun would not turn dark until I died . . .
> If I were to trade in shrouds
> No one would die as long as I lived!

Moses Maimonides (Rambam) (1138–1204) – philosopher, codifier, and physician

'The great eagle', as he was admiringly referred to in later centuries, was born in Cordoba, in Muslim Andalusia (Spain), where in recent times his memory has become a source of local pride and tourist income. In Jewish circles, he is generally known as Rambam, from the initial letters of his name (see box p. 39).

In 1148 Cordoba was taken by the Almohades, who not only suppressed other Islamic groups who did not share their puritanical attitude, but destroyed synagogues and offered Jews the choice of apostasy or death. The family of Maimon fled to Fez (Morocco), where they lived for a few years; Rambam's sensitive *Epistle on Apostasy*, composed in about 1160, evinces great sympathy with and tolerance for those who under duress had conformed outwardly to Islam. In 1165, after failing in their attempt to settle in Crusader Palestine, the family found rest in Egypt, first in Alexandria and eventually in Fostat, old Cairo, under the new Ayyubid dynasty of Saladin.

Rambam devoted himself to studies and writing. By the 1170s he was regarded as Nagid (leader) of the Jews of Cairo, but it remains unclear whether he held an official position. When his brother David, whose commercial activities supported the family, perished at sea, Moses turned to the practice of medicine to support himself and his dependents, becoming private physician to Saladin's vizier Alfadhel. His advice and opinions were sought all over the Jewish world, from Provence to Yemen to Baghdad, and much of his correspondence has been preserved, some of it in the Cairo *geniza* (above, p. 37). He died in Fostat on 13 December 1204 and was mourned by Muslims as well as Jews. He was buried in Tiberias (Palestine).

His *Mishneh Torah*, in Hebrew, is a systematic digest of the whole range of Jewish law, incorporating not only ritual and liturgical matters, and the civil and criminal codes, but regulations on agriculture in the Land of Israel and on Temple building and procedures and ritual purity. Its most remarkable feature is the way he expounds *halakha* in terms of his ethical and philosophical convictions, for instance by interpreting the commandment to love God as including a call to engage in natural science and comprehend the wonders of creation; the short sections on cosmology and medicine are masterpieces of what nowadays would be thought of as popular science writing. He rejects rabbinic laws he considers to be based on superstition, or on belief in demons and magic, and is particularly outspoken in his rejection of astrology.

His philosophical masterpiece is the Judaeo-Arabic *Guide for the Perplexed*, in which like Saadia before him, or the Muslim philosophers Alfarabi and Avicenna to whom he was greatly indebted, he harmonizes religious tradition with philosophy, in his case principally the philosophy of Aristotle. The *Guide* influenced not only Jewish thought, but in Latin translation Christian theologians such as Thomas Aquinas. It aroused controversy in traditional circles even in his own time. Still today the Orthodox, who venerate his *Mishneh Torah* as the pinnacle of halakhic writing, are puzzled by many of the doctrines in the *Guide*; they either ignore it, or read mystical interpretations into it which would have alarmed its author.

Maimonides was one of the first to attempt to formulate a Jewish creed, perhaps because of the need to draw clear lines in the face of Muslim and Christian attempts to convert Jews. His 'thirteen principles of the faith', elaborated in his early Commentary on the Mishna, are listed in Appendix A on p. 136.

Abraham Abulafia (1240–c.1300?) – ecstatic mystic

In 1280, shortly before the Jewish New Year, Abraham Abulafia, prompted by a 'voice', went to Rome to convert Pope Nicholas III. Nicholas was not amused, and gave orders to burn him at the stake. Abulafia, apparently undisturbed, set off for Suriano, where on 22 August he received the news that the pope had died the previous night of an apoplectic fit. On his return to Rome he was imprisoned for a month, but then released.

What sort of Jew, in the thirteenth century, would consider the pope fair game for conversion? Perhaps only one who thought of himself as a prophet. Abulafia, who was born in Saragossa (Spain), led a restless, some might say wild, life. At the age of 18 he journeyed to Acre (Palestine), in the hope of going on to find the legendary river Sambatyon, which roared in torrents throughout the week and rested on the Sabbath (he didn't find it, nor has anyone else since). He then embarked on intensive study, first of the philosophy of Maimonides (too rational), then of the esoteric Kabbala, which was rather more to his taste. Back in Spain in his early thirties he received visions, intensified his mystical study and speculation, and concluded that mastery of the divine names plus rites and ascetic practices were the key to becoming a prophet. He left Spain again, and in 1279 in Patras (Greece) wrote his first prophetic book. He called his method 'prophetic kabbala', and looked down on the 'common' kabbala of the ten sefirot (divine emanations) as a preliminary and inferior grade of knowledge, speculative rather than actually effective.

Not surprisingly, he created disturbances wherever he went. In Sicily he appeared as prophet and Messiah, a fact we glean from a strongly worded letter by Rabbi Solomon ben Adret of Barcelona to the people of Palermo denouncing him. Because of the attacks by ben Adret and others, ecstatic kabbala as taught by Abulafia vanished from Spain after 1280, finding a home in Islamic lands, where it accorded well with Sufi mysticism. Abulafia was all but forgotten, and only now are scholars piecing together his philosophy from unpublished manuscripts strewn through the libraries of Europe.

Moderns like him more than his contemporaries or immediate successors did, perhaps because they don't have to put up with his excesses. 'Before his vision stood the ideal of a unity of faith, the realization of which he strove to bring about.' Abulafia addressed the enlightened, though not the common herd, amongst Christians as well as Jews. His concept of the essential unity of the mystical way, transcending doctrinal differences, is rare in pre-modern Judaism, though appealing today. And modern students of the kabbala have accepted Abulafia's division of the subject. The 'theosophical-theurgic', such as that of the ten sefirot, centres on God and has two aspects; the theoretical understanding of the divine, and the bringing of harmony into the divine realm itself. Ecstatic kabbala, of which Abulafia is himself the principal advocate, centres on the human; it finds supreme value in the mystical experience of the individual, but is not concerned about the effect of this on the inner harmony of the deity.

Graçia Nasi (c.1510–c.1569) – benefactress

At Ash Wednesday in 1391 a fearful outbreak of violence took place against the Jews in Seville. Many were murdered, others were forced to accept baptism. The Golden Age of Spanish Jewry had commenced its decline into oppression, persecution, and expulsion.

Some of the forced converts from 1391 onwards came to accept Christianity. Others secretly cherished Judaism. Many rose to occupy high places in the Church, as bishops and cardinals. The Inquisition, set up to ferret out Christian heresy, was invited to assess the sincerity of the 'New Christians', as these *conversos* were eventually called (some people still use the term *marranos*, from a Castilian word for 'pig'; this should be avoided). Denunciations were easy, and often enough true; confessions and further accusations were extracted by torture, and conviction led to burning at the stake. (The Church still claims it did not burn anyone at the stake. This is true. It tortured victims, often in public, then handed them to the temporal authorities for strangling and burning.)

On the day before Columbus (possibly himself a secret Jew, and certainly indebted to Jewish science and finance for his epic voyage) set sail for 'India', the shorter but more perilous voyages began of the Jews expelled from Spain by Ferdinand and Isabella despite the eloquent pleas of their Jewish chancellor, the great Don Isaac Abravanel (an event described graphically in his own Bible commentary). Some were welcomed to Portugal, to be expelled a few years later in horrific circumstances, their children being wrenched from them and subjected to forced baptism.

In 1536 a papal brief ordered the Inquisition into Portugal. Amongst those who escaped at that time to the less oppressive regime of Antwerp was a wealthy young widow called Beatriz de Luna, whose husband, Diogo Francisco, had amassed a fortune through the spice trade. Like other 'New Christians' her destination of choice was Turkey, but travel to a non-Christian country was not permitted. Had she openly declared her intention, it would have been tantamount to professing Judaism, which even in Antwerp could have led to denunciation, death

4. Medal struck about 1553 in honour of Doña Graçia Nasi, by Pastorino de' Pastorini of Ferrara.

at the stake, and the confiscation of all the family's property. Instead she built up the family business and its international connections and did everything in her power, using trustworthy agents throughout Europe and even in Turkey itself, to help others escape from Portugal and the Inquisition and find their way at least to England or the Netherlands and ultimately to a safe haven where they might proclaim their true faith.

Towards the end of 1544 she moved to Venice, still in Christian guise. In a dramatic development from a family quarrel she was denounced by her sister (later a staunch Jewess) as a Judaizer and imprisoned, only being released when the Sublime Porte intervened on her behalf and the matter threatened to destabilize international relations. At last, in Ferrara in 1550, under the protection of the Duke Ercole II of the House of Este, she was able to throw off the disguise and exchange her 'Marrano' name of Beatriz de Luna for the more Jewish Graçia (= Hannah) of the House of Nasi. The last few years of her life were spent in Constantinople, where she lived in a splendid residence in Galata, overlooking the Bosporus, and continued without interruption her great work of rescuing Iberian Jewry and looking after the poor and destitute. 'Eighty mendicants', we are told, 'sat down each day at her table, and blessed her name'. Nor was she remiss in supporting scholars, publication, and institutes of learning and prayer; already in Ferrara she had supported such ventures as the publication of the 'Ferrara Bible' in Hebrew and Spanish.

Her contemporary Samuel Usque, in his *Consolation for the Tribulations of Israel*, devotes an entire section to Doña Graçia's work in organizing the flight of the refugees from Portugal. His panegyric is by no means excessive:

> Who has seen, as you [people of Israel] have, the Divine mercy reveal itself in human guise, as He has shown and continues to show you for your succour? Who has seen revived the intrinsic piety of Miriam, offering her life to save her brethren? The great prudence of Deborah, in governing her people? That infinite virtue and great sanctity of Esther, in helping those who are persecuted? The much praised strength of the most chaste and magnanimous widow Judith, in delivering those hemmed in by travail? . . . It is she (Doña Graçia Nasi) who aided you with motherly love and heavenly liberality in the dangerous and urgent necessities which you experienced . . . Succouring the multitude of necessitous and miserable poor, refusing no favour even to those who were her enemies . . . In such wise, with her golden arm and heavenly grasp, she raised most of those of this people from the depths of this and

other infinite travail in which they were kept enthralled in Europe by poverty and sin; she brings them to safe lands and does not cease to guide them, and gathers them to the obedience and precepts of their God of old . . . (translated by Cecil Roth)

Baal Shem Tov (c.1700–1760) – Hasidism

Appearances can be deceptive. When you see on your television screen, or on the streets of Brooklyn, London, or Jerusalem, bearded, ear-locked, tieless Jewish men in heavy black hats and frock coats, you might well imagine that they represent the most conservative, traditional wing of Judaism. But the clothes themselves should give you the clue that all is not as it seems. Moses didn't dress like that, nor did Judah the Patriarch or Saadia or Rashi. The clothes, like the popular music of the Hasidic Klezmer bands, would not have been out of place in eighteenth-century Ukraine or Poland, and that is indeed the home of Hasidism, which was perceived at its origins as a revolutionary, populist movement that threatened to undermine established order and tradition.

Baal Shem Tov (BESHT)

The title *Baal Shem* (Hebrew – 'master of the Name') was given to healers who were thought to achieve miraculous cures by writing or uttering letters of the divine names. *Tov* means 'good'. *Baal Shem Tov* may be abbreviated as 'BESHT'.

The founder of the movement was Israel ben Eliezer, more often known as the Baal Shem Tov (see Box) from his reputation as an itinerant healer. Born to aged parents in Podolia (Ukraine), he was orphaned early and grew up in poverty. In his early years he showed no special talents, but was entrusted to gather and bring the children to the Heder, or religious school; even at that stage he would wander into the forests of the Carpathian mountains to meditate amongst nature. He married, and for a time eked out a living as an innkeeper.

Only in his thirties – according to the standard hagiography 'In Praise of the Besht' – did he reveal himself to close disciples as a profound scholar and mystic. As a charismatic healer he attracted a wide following, and inspired people to worship God and keep His commandments in simplicity and with joy. Rather like Jesus he scandalized the orthodox by chatting with women and simple people and by his apparent indifference to the finer points of law.

The movement was carried through Ukraine and Poland by itinerant preachers such as the Maggid of Miedyrzecz, and very soon Hasidim were singing and dancing and even drinking in the synagogues to the dismay of the authorities, and displacing the traditional rabbis with their own 'rebbes'. Their enthusiasm, egalitarianism, and lack of emphasis on traditional scholarship attracted mass following. Soon, there were Hasidic communities each with a hereditary 'Rebbe' (rabbi) or *Tzaddik* ('righteous one') at its head, guiding the faithful and performing miracles. Many of the early sects still thrive and are known by the names of the towns with which they were connected – thus Belzer Hasidim, Gerer Hasidim, Bratslaver Hasidim – and several are still led by 'Rebbes', of whom Menahem Mendel Schneersohn, the 'Lubavitcher Rebbe', had perhaps the highest public profile in recent times.

As Hasidism grew it adjusted to some of the criticisms levelled against it by the 'Mitnagdim' (opponents). Its acolytes became more law-abiding, and more devoted to learning, many Hasidic rabbis being scholars of distinction as well as men of outstanding piety. Unlike the Mitnagdim, though, they attached as much importance to kabbala and mystical studies as to Talmud, and promoted kabbalistic ideas at a popular level; they stressed the immanence rather than the transcendence of God.

The telling of stories is an important element in Hasidic teaching; Martin Buber rewrote many of them in German (English translations of his work are available), making something of the flavour of Hasidism accessible to a wider public.

Though Hasidism endorses traditional Messianic doctrine, it stresses personal rather than national aspects of redemption. Mostly, it has managed to defuse (though never to abandon) messianic expectations; the claim made by followers of the late Lubavitcher Rebbe that he was the Messiah owe more to evangelical Christianity than to Hasidic tradition.

Moses Mendelssohn (1729–86) – Enlightenment

It would be hard to find a greater contrast between two contemporaries within the Jewish world than that between Israel Baal Shem Tov and Moses Mendelssohn. Each, in similar measure but opposite direction, profoundly influenced the subsequent development of Judaism.

Mendelssohn, born in Dessau, journeyed to Berlin, where he privately studied mathematics, philosophy and languages; Jews were excluded from the universities. He was forced to earn a living as a private tutor in the household of a wealthy Jewish silk merchant. Eventually he was befriended by the young liberal German dramatist and critic Gotthold Ephraim Lessing; Lessing is thought to have modelled the hero of his play *Nathan der Weise* on Mendelssohn. The crowning episode of this stage of his life came in 1764, when he was awarded the Berlin Academy's prize for the best essay on the relationship between metaphysical and scientific method; amongst his competitors was Immanuel Kant! Mendelssohn's dialogue *Phädon* (1767), on immortality, earned him the sobriquet of 'the German Socrates'.

In 1769 the Swiss deacon Johann Kaspar Lavater challenged Mendelssohn either to refute Christianity or else to do what 'reason and integrity would otherwise lead him to do', and convert. In his courageous and dignified reply Mendelssohn strongly affirmed his faith in Judaism, and even claimed superiority for that faith on the grounds that it was fundamentally more tolerant than Christianity. He wrote:

> According to the basic principles of my religion I am not to seek to convert anyone not born into our laws . . . Our Rabbis unanimously teach that the written and oral laws which comprise our revealed religion are obligatory upon our nation only . . . We believe the other nations of the earth are directed by God to observe (only) the Law of Nature and the Religion of the Patriarchs. Those who conduct their lives in accordance with this religion of nature and reason are known as 'righteous gentiles' and are 'children of everlasting salvation'. So far are our rabbis from wishing to convert, that they instruct us to dissuade, by earnest remonstrance, any who come forward of their own accord . . .

> If, amongst my contemporaries, there were a Confucius or a Solon, I could consistently with my religious principles, love and admire the great man; the ridiculous thought of converting Confucius or Solon would not enter my head. Convert him indeed! Why? He is not of the Congregation of Jacob, and therefore not subject to my religious laws; as concerns doctrine we should reach a common understanding. Do I think he would be 'saved'? I fancy that whosoever leads men to virtue in this life cannot be damned in the next – nor do I fear to be called to account for this opinion by any august college, as was honest Marmontel by the Sorbonne.

Mendelssohn was an ardent advocate of Jewish civil rights, and a pioneer in denouncing Jewish separatism. He strongly urged his fellow Jews to assimilate, so far as their religion would permit, into German culture and society, and to speak High German rather than Yiddish. His *Biur*, a German translation in Hebrew letters of the Bible, together with a Hebrew commentary, was received as far afield as England with enthusiasm; some traditionalists frowned upon it, though they stopped short of excommunication. He encouraged the setting-up of the Jewish Free School in Bèrlin in 1781, in which secular subjects, French, and German, as well as traditional Talmud and Bible, were taught.

In his philosophical work *Jerusalem* he argued the case for complete separation of Church and State; he opposed both Church ownership of property, and the use (by Church or Synagogue) of the ban of excommunication. He vigorously opposed pantheism, but his own 'religion of nature and reason' verges on the deistic. Mendelssohn distanced himself, as did many contemporary Christians, from credal formulations; even scripture, though he did not express doubts as to its divine origin, was to him 'revealed legislation', free from dogma. 'The spirit of Judaism is freedom in doctrine and conformity in action,' he asserted.

Such ideas were distant from the mainstream of Jewish religious tradition, but they enabled people to continue to make sense of their faith whilst absorbing what they found of value in the Enlightenment. Not only Reform but also Modern Orthodoxy draw heavily on Mendelssohn's pioneering synthesis between tradition and modernity.

Chapter 4
The calendar and festivals

Days and months and years

The key to the Jewish calendar is Nature.

If you woke up one day, far from civilization, with no calendar and no clock, how would you mark the passage of time? As time moved on, how would you celebrate or commemorate events of significance in your life, such as the day you were born, the day you survived shipwreck, the harvest you gathered?

You would notice the sun rise and set, and you would observe that it reached its highest point in the sky just in the middle of the day. But you would not be able to fix midnight. So, your days would start either at sunrise or at sunset, or thereabouts. In fact, both ways survive in the Jewish calendar. Temple procedures were scheduled into a day that began at dawn. For all other purposes, day began at nightfall. That is why, for instance, the Sabbath commences not at midnight on Friday or Saturday, but a little before sunset on Friday night – exact times vary through seasons and latitudes, and are posted in the Jewish press.

This simple fact leads to great consequences. If the Sabbath began at midnight, few people would be around to notice. But, as it begins earlier, before people take their evening meal, Friday night has become one of the great Jewish social institutions. People attend prayers in the synagogue, with joyful psalms and hymns, and return to a brightly lit home and a festive table to recite the *kiddush* blessing over a cup of wine and to break bread together; grace and hymns are sung, and family and visitors are joined in a bond of spiritual warmth. Even those who don't attend the synagogue, or are not particularly religious, still have a family gathering on Friday night. If family values and the warmth of belonging to family and community persist in Judaism, this is largely due to the peace and harmony which are felt in so many homes as the candles are lit at the beginning of the Sabbath.

So much for days beginning at sunset rather than midnight. What about months and years?

Nature is the key. A month (the word comes from 'moon') is the time the moon takes to wax and wane – just over 29½ days. A year is the time the seasons take to complete their round (nowadays we know it depends on the earth's orbit around the sun) – just under 365¼ days. It was very inconvenient of nature to fix things this way, because there is no way to divide 365¼ by 29½ without remainder. Muslims gave up on the solar year and have a year of twelve lunar months, losing eleven or so days each year in relation to everybody else's year; their festivals can't be nature-based, since they move across the seasons. In the Western, Christian-based calendar, years correspond to the seasons, but months no longer relate to the phases of the moon. The calendar adopted by the rabbis makes the best of both worlds, but there is a price to pay for sticking to nature; months vary between twenty-nine and thirty days, years vary between twelve and thirteen months, and there are seven leap years (that is, years with thirteen months) every nineteen years. Complicated, but it works. New Moon is celebrated, and so are the changing seasons (see Table 4.1).

In Bible times the New Moon was a festival of considerable importance – the woman of Shunem who dashed off to Elisha the prophet when her son collapsed puzzled her husband because it was 'neither new moon

TABLE 4.1. Hebrew months

Hebrew	Equivalent (months overlap)
Nisan	March–April
Iyar	April–May
Sivan	May–June
Tammuz	June–July
Ab	July–August
Elul	August–September
Tishri	September–October
Heshvan	October–November
Kislev	November–December
Tebet	December–January
Shevat	January–February
Adar	February–March
2nd Adar	*In leap year only.*

nor sabbath' (2 Kgs. 4: 23) – but it was played down in later Judaism. Still, in some communities during the Middle Ages women abstained from work on the New Moon. Jewish feminists noticed this medieval hint and have built on it to reclaim *Rosh Hodesh* (the New Moon) as a women's festival of renewal, on which they read liturgies that celebrate aspects of women's spirituality. There are now many *Rosh Hodesh* associations around the world, set up to encourage women's prayer and religious education.

The Pilgrim festivals

Three of the most popular Bible-based festivals are known as 'pilgrim' or 'foot' festivals, because in ancient times pilgrims used to travel to the Temple in Jerusalem to celebrate. Philo of Alexandria, the great Jewish philosopher who died early in the first century, wrote a vivid eye-witness account of the scene: 'Countless multitudes from countless cities come, some over land, others over sea, from east and west and north and

5. A Jewish family in England discussing Torah at a meal in the Succah on the festival of Tabernacles (Succot).

south at every feast. They take the temple for their port as a general haven and safe refuge from the bustle and turmoil of life, and there they seek to find calm weather, and, released from the cares whose yoke has been heavy upon them from their earliest years, to enjoy a brief breathing-space in scenes of genial cheerfulness.'

The three Pilgrim festivals have in common the theme of joy in God's presence: 'And you shall rejoice on your festivals'; present yourself in the 'chosen place' (Jerusalem) bearing your 'gift' for God (Deut. 16: 14–16). The festive joy is traditionally expressed in feasting with meat and drink, and with the purchase of new garments for the women. It is a joy which is only complete when allied with concern for the needy; as the verse continues, 'with . . . the strangers, orphans and widows among you'; hence, still today, the festivals are times when people respond most generously to charitable appeals.

Each of the festivals has a historical, a spiritual, and an agricultural, meaning; the mystics delve beyond these into layers of hidden, inner meanings (see Table 4.2).

Synagogue services tend on the whole to be fairly sedate, but there are exceptions. On 14 October 1663 the English diarist Samuel Pepys took it into his head to visit, for the second time, the synagogue at Creechurch Lane, London. What he saw astonished him. Pandemonium appeared to be let loose, as grey-bearded men holding Torah scrolls pranced and cavorted about the synagogue like young goats. Pepys had unwittingly chosen to indulge his inquisitiveness on the day of Simchat Torah, the great celebration at the end of Succot when the reading of the annual Torah cycle is completed and recommenced, and joyful processions of men circle around the *bima* (central platform) dancing with the Torah in their arms.

Festival celebrations are as much a matter for the home as for the synagogue. Undoubtedly the most popular and fascinating of these celebrations is the Passover meal, or Seder. Its origins lie far back in the Temple ritual of the Passover lamb, which was slaughtered on the afternoon of the Eve of Passover and eaten ceremonially in the home in the evening, the first night of the festival. The Hallel (Pss. 113–18) was recited in the Temple, and has been transferred to the Seder meal. There is no longer a sacrificial lamb, but both *matza* (unleavened bread) and bitter herbs feature prominently.

The evening's procedure, however, is built around *haggada*, which means 'telling the story'. *Haggada* is also the name of the book in which the service is printed; many Jews pride themselves on their collections of *haggadot* (Hebrew feminine plural – *ot*), some of which are beautifully printed and illustrated, and many of which contain explanations and up-to-date commentaries. The Bible actually says, 'And you shall tell your son on that day, saying, "It is on account of what the Lord did for me when I came out of Egypt" ' (Exod. 13: 8), and it is around this commandment that the Seder service has evolved.

TABLE 4.2. The Pilgrim festivals and their meanings

Name of festival	Historical	Spiritual	Agricultural
Pesach (Passover) spring	Commemorates the Exodus of the Israelites from slavery in Egypt	God is the Redeemer; from being slaves to Pharaoh in Egypt, the Israelites became the servants of God alone	The festival of spring, of re-growth, of the earliest cereal harvest, barley
Shavuot (Pentecost) early summer	Is the day on which God gave the Ten Commandments at Mount Sinai, as the terms of his Covenant with Israel	The Redemption from Egypt was complete only when its *spiritual* dimension was achieved by Revelation of the Torah at Sinai	Marks the late cereal harvest (wheat) and the first fruits
Succot (Tabernacles) autumn	God protected the Israelites in the desert: 'So that your generations should know that I made the Israelites dwell in booths when I brought them out of the land of Egypt' (Lev. 23: 43)	God is our Protector; this is symbolized as we leave our homes and dwell in simple booths (*succot*)	The final Harvest Festival of the year

6. Children in a Jerusalem kindergarten learn to celebrate the Passover Seder (1971).

The Seder is a participatory event. Everyone joins in reading, discussion, and songs. One of the highlights, near the beginning, is the 'four questions', sung in Hebrew by the youngest child, who may well have spent weeks training to do this and looking forward excitedly to being allowed up so late with the grown-ups. Few Jews ever forget the words *ma nishtana ha-layla ha-zé* . . . 'Why is this night different from all other nights . . .', which in so many cases bring back to them happy memories of a childhood nurtured in a loving family circle.

Since rabbinic times it has been customary to drink four cups of wine at the Seder. They represent four stages of redemption, from the Exodus itself (prior to the meal) to the Messiah (after the meal). Some have a fifth cup, or simply place an extra cup of wine on the table 'for the prophet ELIJAH'.

One of the joys of a well-run Seder is the participation of all present in the discussion, whether derived from published commentaries or spontaneous and original. Several recent editions have attempted to apply the lessons of the *haggada* to contemporary issues; who are the nations or marginalized groups in contemporary society, and by what means are they to be 'liberated'?

Domestic preparations for Passover are very intense, and dominated by the obligation to remove all *hametz* (leaven) from one's possession prior to the festival, in accordance with the Bible's instructions (Exod. 12: 15–20, 13: 7); hence it is a time of thorough spring cleaning. Special utensils and foods are required for the festival, free from *hametz*. Jewish grocers, and nowadays many general supermarkets, supply a wide range of foods approved for Passover use; Jewish cookery books usually carry a selection of Passover recipes, in which the place of flour is taken by matza meal or potato flour.

Days of Awe

Not all Jewish festivals are days of joy. The New Year (Rosh Hashana) and Day of Atonement (Yom Kippur) are serious – though not sad – occasions, marking the beginning and end of the Ten Days of Penitence. The Ten Days themselves round off the *yamim noraim*, or Days of Awe, a forty-day penitential period which begins a month before the New Year. (A little bit like Lent but in the autumn, not the spring.)

At the New Year's Eve feast (remember, the day begins with the previous evening) people eat foods symbolizing sweetness, blessings, and abundance. They dip the bread in honey instead of the customary salt, and after breaking bread eat a piece of apple dipped in honey and pray, 'May it be Your will to renew for us a good and sweet year.'

The Morning Service is a long one – from four to six hours – but well attended, even if many drift in late. Prayers centre on the image of God as creator, king, and judge, who exercises forgiveness and compassion towards those who turn to him and seek his mercy. The most distinctive observance of the day is the sounding of the *shofar*, or ram's horn, at intervals through the service. It is not an easy instrument to sound correctly owing to its irregular bore and poorly shaped embouchure, but at its best it stirs to penitence and fulfils the words of the prophet, 'Shall the horn be sounded in the city and the people not tremble!' (Amos 3: 6).

Early in the first century Philo noted that Yom Kippur was observed 'not only by the pious and holy but by those who never act religiously in the rest of their life'. This is still true. For at least part of the day (prayers continue throughout the day) synagogues are full to overflowing. Not all of those who attend are eagerly seeking forgiveness of sin, or engaging solemnly in soul-searching and penitence, tempered by confident faith in God's mercy and compassion on frail humanity. That is indeed what the day is about, and what the pious are about. For many people, however, putting in a brief appearance at the synagogue on Yom Kippur is a statement of Jewish identity rather than a religious commitment.

But it is a remarkable way to demonstrate identity, especially if – as is often the case even with the minimally religious – it is combined with fasting. For on Yom Kippur not only work is forbidden, as on the Sabbath, but there are five *innuyim*, or forms of self-discipline: the prohibitions of eating and drinking (counted as one), anointing with oils, sexual relations, washing (for pleasure), and wearing leather shoes.

Teshuva (penitence) is not only the theme of Yom Kippur but a leading concept in Judaism. It is a 'return' (the literal translation of the word) to God, and consists of the recognition of sin, regret and confession, and renewed commitment to the right path. No sacrifice or intermediary is required to complete the process, which depends on God's grace alone. In the formal words of the Mishna (see p. 34):

> *Teshuva* (penitence) atones (immediately) for minor sins, both positive and negative, but if a serious sin has been committed it hangs in suspense until Yom Kippur comes and atones. If someone says, 'I shall sin and repent, I shall sin and repent', he is not given an opportunity to repent. If someone says, 'I will sin and Yom Kippur will atone', Yom Kippur does not atone. Yom Kippur atones for sins between man and God, but it does not atone for offences against another person until reconciliation has been effected.

Much is made of *Kol Nidrei*, which opens the synagogue service for Yom Kippur Eve. Though the Aramaic words are a prosaic formula for the annulment of inadvertent vows, the deeply moving melody, and the solemn atmosphere as the whole congregation gathers before God in awe and expectation, sedately dressed in their finest clothes, combine to generate one of the most emotionally charged moments of the Jewish year.

7. The *shofar* is generally made from the horn of a ram or an ibex; it may not be made from the horn of a cow or bull, for this would bring to mind the sin of worshipping the Golden Calf.

The final service the following day, as the fast ends, is *Neʿilah* (the 'closing of the gates'); worshippers are stirred to make the most of this final hour when the gates of heaven remain wide open. It culminates on an emotional high, as *Avinu Malkenu* ('our father, our king') is chanted, the unity of God is declared by the congregation in unison, and a final blast is sounded on the *shofar*.

So much for major festivals. There are also a number of minor ones, of which the most popular are Chanukah, Purim, the New Year for Trees, and Israel Independence Day.

Chanukah celebrates the re-dedication of the Temple by the Hasmoneans in about 165 BCE. This is how the Talmud describes its origin:

TABLE 4.3. A Jewish calendar for 2004/5
Since the Jewish New Year is in the fall Jewish years overlap those on the civil calendar. 5765 AM, a leap year, runs from 16 September 2004 to 3 October 2005

Civil date	Jewish date	Occasion
16/17 Sept. 2004	1 and 2 Tishri	New Year
19 Sept. 2004	4 Tishri	Fast of Gedaliah
23 Sept. 2004	10 Tishri	Day of Atonement
30 Sept. 2004	15 Tishri	Sukkot, First Day
7 Oct. 2004	22 Tishri	Shemini Atzeret
8 Dec. 2004	25 Kislev	First Day of Hanukah
22 Dec. 2004	10 Tevet	Fast of 10th Tevet
25 Jan. 2005	15 Shevat	New Year for trees
24 Mar. 2005	13 Adar	Fast of Esther
25 Mar. 2005	14 Adar	Purim
24 Apr. 2005	15 Nisan	Pesach, First Day
30 Apr. 2005	21 Nisan	Pesach, Seventh Day
13 June 2005	6 Sivan	Shavuot
24 July 2005	17 Tammuz	Fast of 17th Tammuz
14 Aug. 2005	9 Ab	Fast of 9th Ab

The following additional festival days are observed in the diaspora:

1 Oct. 2004	16 Tishri	Sukkot, Second Day
8 Oct. 2004	23 Tishri	Simchat Torah
25 Apr. 2005	16 Nisan	Pesach, Second Day
1 May 2005	22 Nisan	Pesach, Final Day
14 June 2005	7 Sivan	Shavuot, Second Day

Eight days of Chanukah commence on the twenty-fifth of Kislev, and one may not eulogise or fast on them. For when the Greeks entered the Temple they defiled all the oils in the Temple, but when the Hasmoneans became strong and defeated them they searched, and found only one cruse of oil remaining with the High Priest's seal, and there was sufficient in it for one day only. A miracle occurred and they lit from it for eight days. In a later year they fixed these days as a festival for praise and thanksgiving.

By focusing attention on the 'miracle of the oil', which is not mentioned in the other sources, the rabbis transformed the festival from thanksgiving for a military victory to a celebration of the triumph of light over darkness; in the words of Zechariah, 'Not by might, nor by power, but by My Spirit, says the Lord of hosts' (Zech. 4: 6).

On each of the eight nights of the festival a light is kindled 'to advertise the miracle'. One light on the first night, two on the second, and so on, until eight are kindled on the final night. Oil is preferred to wax candles, and nowadays most people have a *menora*, or *hannukiya* (candelabrum), specially for Chanukah. Many of these candelabra are beautifully designed, and executed in precious metal.

Purim celebrates the rescue of the Jews from the threat of extermination under Ahasuerus, king of Persia, as recounted in the biblical Book of Esther. The *megilla* (Hebrew parchment scroll of Esther) is read publicly both evening and morning following the respective services. There is a widespread custom of banging and noise-making whenever the name of the villain, Haman, is read out. The more censorious object to this, stressing that every word must be heard clearly.

The day has a carnival atmosphere, often expressed in dressing-up, carnival processions, and even a satirical *Purim Spiel*. Following Esther 9: 22, alms are distributed to the needy, people send gifts of food to each other, and there is general feasting and merriment. Opinions vary as to the commendable degree of intoxication.

The New Year for Trees is mentioned in the Talmud, but it is only with the 'return to the Land' in modern times that it has become a popular festival. In Israel in particular *Tu biShevat*, as it is known, is marked by a school holiday and tree-planting ceremonies. There is also a widespread custom of eating fifteen fruits, corresponding to the date of the month; fruits of the land of Israel are favoured.

The designation of 5 Iyar (late April/May) in the religious calendar as Yom Ha-Atzma ʿut (Israel Independence Day) has not been without controversy, whether from political or religious reasons. Nevertheless, many Jews both inside and outside Israel celebrate, reciting special psalms and prayers as well as organizing social events.

Fast days

In addition to Yom Kippur there are five public fast days in the year, the most important of which is 9 Ab *(Tisha b'Ab)*, commemorating the destruction of both Temples as well as other tragedies. Both Yom Kippur and *Tisha b'Ab* are twenty-five-hour fasts, when nothing may be eaten or drunk from just before sunset on one day until after nightfall on the following day; there are, of course, dispensations for those for whom fasting is difficult or dangerous. The other fast days run only from daybreak until nightfall.

Chapter 5
The spiritual life – prayer, meditation, Torah

Here is a story from the Talmud. Some explanatory notes are put in square brackets; you are left to sort out for yourself who 'he' is each time the pronoun is used. Don't be surprised that the prophet Elijah figures in the story; though he ascended to heaven in a fiery chariot about a thousand years before the Talmud was written, he does come back now and then to guide and encourage the learned and devout. Even in our own sceptical days there are people to whom he is said to have revealed himself. 'Destined for the World to Come', incidentally, means much the same as the Christian expression 'saved'.

Rabbi Baroka of Hoza'a used to go to Lefet Market, and Elijah often kept him company. He asked him, 'Is there anyone in this market who is destined for the World to Come?' He replied, 'No!'

After a while he saw a man who wore black shoes and did not wear a blue thread on his clothes [i.e. he was not dressed in the Jewish manner]. He said, 'That man is destined for the World to Come.'

He ran after him, and said to him, 'What do you do?' He said, 'Go away today and come back tomorrow'. The next day he said to him, 'What do you do?' He said to him, 'I am a prison guard. I confine the men and women separately and put my bed between them, so that they don't do anything forbidden [by the Torah]. When I see that the heathen take a fancy to a Jewish girl I go out of my way to protect her. One day there was a betrothed girl on whom the heathen set their eyes. I took the lees of the red wine and threw it on her skirt and they thought she was menstruating [and so left her alone].'

'Why don't you put [blue] fringes on your clothes, and why do you wear black shoes?'

'Because I go amongst the heathen and I don't want them to know that I am a Jew, so that when they make a decree against the Jews I can inform the rabbis, who then pray and avert the decree.'

'Why is it that when I asked you what you do you told me to go away and come back the next day?'

He said, 'Just then they made a decree, and I said first I must go and inform the rabbis, so that they might pray about it.'

Meanwhile, two brothers came by. He said to him, 'They also are destined for the World to Come.'

He went to them and said to them, 'What do you do?' They said to him, 'We are clowns. We bring cheer to the downhearted. Or else, when we see two people quarrel, we go and make peace between them.'

This curious tale is aimed at people who think they know what it means to be 'spiritual'. The 'heroes of the spirit', Elijah shows the conventional rabbi Baroka, are not the ostentatiously pious, not even the learned and devout like Baroka himself (who was obviously fishing for a compliment he did *not* receive from the prophet). They may appear to be quite ordinary individuals, not even religious in a conventional sense, whose quiet deeds enhance the quality of life around them – the carers, the compassionate, those who use their talents to ease the burdens of humanity.

All this seems a long way from the Bible's command to spirituality: 'You shall be holy, for I the Lord am holy' (Lev. 19: 2). But is holiness to be found only in fasting and prayer and 'spiritual' exercises? Evidently not – indeed, most of what follows in the chapter in Leviticus has to do with social behaviour, and fasting and prayer are not mentioned. 'Know him in all your ways' (Pro. 3: 6) expresses the way spirituality is understood in Jewish tradition; *every* aspect of life, not just the performance of 'religious' duties, should be the vehicle for devotion to God. True spirituality, or godliness, is found in everyday social relationships as well as in prayer, learning, or ascetic practices.

Nevertheless, prayer is a vital concern in Judaism, and one of the major forms in which spirituality is expressed. Equal in rank, perhaps even higher, is learning. Both are comprehended in *teshuva* 'penitence', the 'return' to God who is our home.

What is prayer?

The Bible records numerous instances of individual prayer; one of the finest is Solomon's prayer at the dedication of the Temple (1 Kgs. 8: 22–53). The Psalms include collective as well as individual prayers; they have been described as the Prayer Book of the Second Temple. Many of them retain their freshness to this day and continue to inspire Christian as well as Jewish worship.

Perhaps because prayer is assumed to be a normal human activity, the Bible has no explicit 'commandment' to pray. The rabbis nevertheless discovered one in the words of Deuteronomy (10: 20): 'the Lord your God – you must serve him.' For prayer is 'service' – the 'service of the heart', in contrast with service through sacrifice in the Temple; the verse teaches that we should serve God through daily prayer. As Maimonides (1138–1204) put it: 'a person [of either sex] should entreat and pray each day, and declare the praises of the Holy One, blessed be he, then petition for his needs . . . and afterwards render praise and

8. The Synagogue in Bevis Marks, London, was built in 1701 to replace the Synagogue in Creechurch Lane. It is the oldest extant Synagogue in Britain and still in regular use.

thanks to the Lord for the good things he has bestowed upon him, each according to his ability.'

In their discussion of prayer the rabbis of the Talmud introduced the concept of *kavvana* ('direction', 'intention'), or inwardness. They interpreted Hannah's prayer for a child (1 Sam. 1) as the prototype of sincere, spontaneous prayer; from Hannah we learn that prayer demands *inner* commitment, the heart rather than the lips. Prayer is not just words; it is, in the words of Psalms, an 'outpouring of the soul', a 'cry from the depths'.

There are many levels of *kavvana*. The Lithuanian rabbi Hayyim Soloveitchik (1853–1917) distinguished between *kavvana* in the simple sense of comprehending the words one is uttering, and *kavvana* as the conscious awareness of being in God's presence and addressing him. The latter, Soloveitchik maintains, is of the essence of prayer; to utter words, however meaningful in themselves, without that profound sense of awe and mystery, is not to pray.

Invocation, praise, thanksgiving, petition (for oneself and others), confession, and appeal for forgiveness, govern the content of prayer.

To whom are prayers directed? The fifth of Maimonides' *Thirteen Principles of the Faith* (see Appendix A) states: 'It is right to pray to the Creator, but to no other being.' He did not approve of mystics who on occasion addressed prayer to angels, or to aspects of the *Shekhina* (divine presence), rather than 'direct' to the infinite Creator.

The Zohar, the crowning achievement of Spanish kabbala (late thirteenth century), conceives of prayer as a Jacob's ladder joining earth to heaven: 'And when prayer reaches that firmament, the twelve gates of the firmament are opened, and over the twelfth gate stands an appointed angel called Anael who is in charge of many hosts and many camps, and when the prayer ascends that angel arises and addresses each gate with the words, "Open your heads, O you gates . . ." (Ps. 24), and all the gates open and the prayer enters through them.' Angels on high are stirred to intercede, barriers are overcome, the Lower and the Higher worlds are united.

Prayer is essentially a private communion between the individual and his or her God, and not bound up with the synagogue; the formal Orders of Service are recited wherever one may be. But congregational prayer adds a significant dimension of spirituality, for the *Shekhina* (divine Presence) rests upon the 'camp of Israel', the assembly of the faithful. Therefore, the regular Orders of Service should be recited, if possible, with a *minyan* (quorum) of participants, defined in tradition as ten or more male Jews of the age of 13 or over. It is preferable, though not essential, to pray in a synagogue; better still, in a *Bet ha-Midrash*, where the Torah is regularly studied, and which therefore has greater sanctity than a place of 'mere' prayer or public assembly.

The Talmud records at least one instance in which a woman's prayer is superior to that of her husband. However, it relegates women to the 'private' sphere, so that they do not make up the prayer quorum and are not obliged to attend a public place of worship. Special women's prayers in Yiddish, called *techines*, with a characteristic spirituality, developed for private use, perhaps as early as the fifteenth century. The non-Orthodox branches of Judaism (see Chapter 7) have, to varying degrees, given women equal status with men in the synagogue. Since the 1980s Orthodox women-only services have been developed along similar lines to the standard services, though not without controversy.

Does prayer work?

Is prayer 'effective'? Does it *work*? The bitter experiences of the Holocaust led many to deny the traditional concept of an 'interventionist' God; God had evidently not intervened in response to the prayers of his people to save them from this terrible catastrophe. Even before the Holocaust some people had been persuaded by scientific and philosophical arguments that, contrary to traditional teaching, God did not intervene directly in human affairs.

Traditionalists nevertheless still believe that God modifies external reality in response to prayer. Others stress the *indirect* effects of prayer; prayer influences external events through psychological processes, including the phenomenon of the 'self-fulfilling prophecy'. Yet reality is not that simple. Even if it is not possible to demonstrate scientifically that prayer changes external reality, the believer may well claim that he or she experiences God's presence in events in the external world.

Prayer undoubtedly modifies the *internal* reality of the one who prays. Indeed, the standard Hebrew term *tefilla* (prayer) derives from a root which means 'to judge', and hence conveys the meaning of self-examination, or introspection. In prayer, one comes to a better understanding of oneself and achieves spiritual development. But many find this an inadequate account of prayer. Abraham Joshua Heschel (1907–71) dismissed it as 'religious solipsism', equating prayer with mere auto-suggestion, and he questioned whether it was therapeutically sound to pray 'as if' God was listening, whilst at the same time denying that He did.

The liturgy

The Psalmist prayed seven times a day (Ps. 119: 164), and Daniel, in Babylon, three times (Dan. 6: 11). Though some scholars demur, it seems certain that Jewish prayer, communal as well as private, separate from Temple worship, was established well before the Romans destroyed the Temple in the year 70.

Still, it was not until about the year 100 that the attempt was made to regulate and define the orders of prayer. The great pioneer of liturgy was Gamaliel II, head of the School at Yavné, near Jerusalem, and effective leader of the Jews. This was at about the same time as Christians were formulating a basic liturgy; perhaps both Jewish and Christian leaders saw the fixed liturgy as a means of defining their faith and promoting 'religious correctness' ideas amongst their followers.

At any rate, Gamaliel's liturgy has determined the form and much of the content of Jewish prayer, Reform as well as Orthodox, to the

The Three Daily Services

Maariv (Aravit)	evening
Shacharit	morning
Mincha	afternoon

present day. There are three daily Orders of Service: *Maariv* (or *Aravit*) in the evening; *Shacharit* in the morning, *Mincha* in the afternoon. On Sabbaths and festivals *Musaf* ('Additional Service') is added following *Shacharit*, on the Day of Atonement also *Ne'ilah* (the 'closing of the gates').

The services are built around two major prayers. One is the *Shema* (accent the 'a'), which consists of three scriptural readings, opening with the declaration of God's Unity. The other is the *Amida* (= 'standing'), or *Shemone Esreh* (= 'eighteen' – the original number of its paragraphs), consisting of praise, petitions, and thanksgiving.

Shema is said at *Maariv* and *Shacharit*, but not at the afternoon service; *Amida* is said at all three.

Gamaliel defined no more than the beginnings and ends of blessings, leaving the prayer leader or individual worshipper to improvise on the set theme. His prayers were brief, and in simple Hebrew, though it was permissible to pray in the vernacular.

Public reading of the Torah was already well established before the time of Gamaliel II, but there was no fixed lectionary nor did he introduce one. The system now more or less universal amongst Jews is that, beginning and ending on the feast of Simchat Torah, the Five Books of Moses (Genesis, Exodus, Leviticus, Numbers, and Deuteronomy) are read publicly in the synagogue in an annual cycle on Sabbath mornings from a handwritten parchment scroll known as a *Sefer Torah*. There are, in addition, many other regular liturgical readings from most parts of the Bible.

Attitude in prayer

The *Amida* prayer is said quietly, standing, in a reverent attitude, feet together, hands folded over heart, facing Jerusalem; at four points you bow slightly. Correct bodily position is not essential to prayer, but concentration is; in sickness, or when travelling in a situation where standing would disturb concentration, you sit, and if you are too agitated to focus your mind you should not attempt the statutory prayers.

The School of Hillel ruled that *Shema* might be recited 'in whatever position one may be' – that is, no special position should be adopted. As you commit yourself to the Unity of God in the first verse ('Hear, O Israel! the Lord is our God. The Lord is One!'), you should keep still, closing your eyes and covering them with your hands in intense concentration. Daniel (Dan. 6: 11) knelt at prayer, and kneeling and prostration took place in the Temple, but are no longer Jewish practice. Kneeling and prostration are confined in the synagogue to the *Alenu* prayer in the Additional Service for the New Year and Day of Atonement, and to the recital of the Temple Service on the latter.

The first paragraph of the *Shema* (Deut. 6: 4–9)

Hear, O Israel! the Lord is our God. The Lord is One!

Blessed be His name, whose glorious kingdom is for ever and ever.

And you shall love the Lord your God with all your heart, with all your soul, and with all your strength. And these words, which I command you today, shall be upon your heart. And you shall teach them to your children, and speak of them, when you sit in your house, when you walk by the way, and when you lie down and when you rise. And you shall bind them as a sign on your hands, and they shall be ornaments between your eyes. And you shall write them on the doorposts of your house and upon your gates.

Poets and singers of the synagogue

Hebrew liturgical poetry has deep roots in Scripture itself – for instance, in the Psalms. The Palestinian school of *piyyut* (the word comes from the same Greek word as the English 'poet') flourished already before the Arab conquest of Palestine in the seventh century. Best known of its poets was Eleazar Kallir, whose compositions still figure prominently in the Orthodox liturgy. His innovative style has complex patterns of rhyme, acrostic, and refrain, and is full of neologisms and strange-sounding grammatical forms, though there are fine examples of a simpler style of writing.

Here are two contrasting examples of Hebrew liturgical poetry. First, a *seliha*, or penitential hymn, composed by the poet/philosopher Solomon ibn Gabirol (eleventh century) in Muslim Spain:

> *I am appalled and in deep torment; on the day my effrontery is recalled –*
> *   what can I say to my Lord?*
> *I am desolate and speechless; when I remember my guilt – I am ashamed and*
> *   confounded.*
> *My days waste in futility; because of the shame of my youth, there is no peace*
> *   within me . . .*
> *When my sin vexes me, my mind reassures me: 'Let us fall into the hand of*
> *   the Lord' [cf. 2 Sam. 24: 14].*
> *Turn from the seat of your dwelling, and open your gates to me, for there is*
> *   none beside you.*
> *O my rock, protect me! Deliver me from my sin, and teach me your Torah . . .*
> *Forgive our sins, and pay no heed to (the sins of) our youth, for our days are*
> *   but a shadow.*

Next we have the first four verses and the final verse of the poem 'Lekha Dodi' ('Come, my friend') composed around 1540 by the kabbalist Solomon Alkabetz. The poem, in which the Sabbath is personified as Bride and Queen, is sung today in almost all rites, both Orthodox and

Reform, at the Friday evening service for the Inauguration of the Sabbath. It reminds us that the Sabbath itself is one of the great spiritual experiences of Judaism, open to every man, woman and child.

> Come, my friend, to meet the Bride, let us receive the Sabbath!
> The One God declared 'observe' and 'remember' as one word
> The Lord is one and his name is one; name, glory and praise!
>> Come my friend . . .
> Come, let us go to meet the Sabbath, for she is the fount of blessing
> Cast for ever from the beginning, final deed in pristine thought.
>> Come my friend . . .
> Sanctuary of the king, royal dwelling, arise from your overthrow!
> Too long have you dwelt in the vale of tears; He will have compassion on
>   you!
>> Come my friend . . .
> My people, shake free of the dust, don your beautiful robes,
> Draw near to my soul, redeem it through the son of Jesse of Bethlehem!
>> Come my friend . . .
> Come in peace, diadem of your husband, in joy and gladness,
> Come O bride, come O bride, amongst the faithful of the special people
>> Come my friend . . .

Little is known of the music of ancient times, though some elements are preserved in the traditional cantillation of the Torah and the older *nusach*, or forms of reading, for some of the prayers. At some time in the Middle Ages the art of the *hazzan*, or prayer-leader, came into being (the term itself is much older, but the role changed), his task being to enhance the beauty of public devotions; larger synagogues nowadays usually boast a professional *hazzan* as well as a rabbi.

Salomone de' Rossi, in Mantua, introduced Italian Renaissance vocal counterpoint into the music of the Synagogue. Since the eighteenth century Hasidim have adopted East European folk-music into the Synagogue, and in the nineteenth the Austrian Salomon Sulzer and the

9. Archaeological excavations have demonstrated that the prohibition against graven images did not inhibit Jews from artistic embellishment of their Synagogues. This sixth-century mosaic unearthed at a Synagogue in Gaza portrays King David playing his harp.

German Louis Lewandowski, who was the first Jewish student of the Prussian Royal Academy of Arts and the first Synagogue choirmaster in modern times, introduced mixed choir, organ, and a Mendelssohnian style; the Orthodox rejected the mixed choir and organ. In the twentieth century several Jewish composers of note, such as Darius Milhaud and Ernest Bloch, have written for the Synagogue.

Whilst the Synagogue has nurtured its own traditions, its music has constantly been influenced by surrounding styles and tastes; the musically educated worshipper can unravel much of Jewish history simply by listening to the tunes! Music, like architecture and the decorative arts, forms an essential part of the spiritual expression of Judaism.

Love of God; meditation, contemplation; pietists

One of the most widespread half-truths about Judaism is that it lacks 'religious orders', such as the monastic orders of the Church. True, there are no Jewish nuns and monks. However, there has been no shortage throughout the centuries of trends, movements, and élite associations devoted to specific forms of spirituality.

Rabbinic Judaism itself was born in such a movement – that of the *haverim*, 'friends', who in the first century formed associations dedicated to strengthening observance of the laws of tithe and purity; rather like some of the Dead Sea Scroll groups, they would take a meal together 'in purity', as in the presence of God in his Temple.

Then there were the circles of the so-called 'Chariot' and 'Hekhalot' mystics, perhaps as early as the third century, whose hymns celebrate the 'heavenly ascent' as the ultimate spiritual experience.

In twelfth-century Egypt a Jewish Sufi movement developed, combining mystical doctrines with spiritual and ascetic exercises. The recent publication of Abraham Maimonides' *Compendium for the Servants of God* and Obadiah Maimonides' *Treatise of the Pool* have brought into sharp focus this movement of *Hasidim*, or 'pious ones'; Abraham was a son, and Obadiah a grandson, of Moses Maimonides.

Far away in Western Europe at much the same time another movement of *Hasidim*, the *Hasidei Ashkenaz* ('German pietists'), with a strong emphasis on mysticism and martyrdom, was formed. Here, in Israel Zangwill's translation, are some verses from the 'Hymn of Glory' composed by one of their leading members, Judah he-Hasid, in which the mystical thirst for intimacy with God is tempered with the philosophical realization that no one can truly grasp His nature:

> Sweet hymns shall be my chant and woven songs,
> For Thou art all for which my spirit longs –
> To be within the shadow of Thy hand
> And all thy mystery to understand.
> The while Thy glory is upon my tongue,
> My inmost heart with love of Thee is wrung . . .
> I have not seen Thee, yet I tell Thy praise,
> Nor known Thee, yet I image forth Thy ways
> For by Thy seers' and servants' mystic speech
> Thou didst Thy sov'ran splendour darkly teach.
> And from the grandeur of Thy work they drew
> The measure of Thy inner greatness, too.
> They told of Thee, but not as Thou must be,
> Since from Thy work they tried to body Thee . . .

Later Jewish 'spiritual' movements include the mystics of sixteenth-century Safed (Palestine), the Ukrainian Hasidism of the eighteenth century, to which today's *Hasidim* belong, and the *Musar* movement of Israel Salanter, with its strong emphasis on ethical self-criticism.

Learning

The most universal, accessible, and distinctive form of Jewish spirituality is Torah study. Of Jonathan son of Uzziel, the greatest disciple of Hillel (early first century), it is related that when he sat and learned Torah so great was the fire of his spiritual passion that if a bird flew overhead it would burst into flame. The words of Torah are as full of joy as on the day that they were given at Sinai.

In the *yeshiva* (nowadays there are similar institutes for women) young men – most of them *not* pursuing a rabbinical vocation – are introduced to traditional Torah study, with its devout intensity. From the *yeshiva* the ideal spills out into the life of ordinary people, who will attend *shiurim* (lessons, lectures) early in the morning before daily prayer, or late at night after work, or whenever they can snatch time in the day, and will learn regularly with a friend, their friendship deepened by a spiritual bond.

Let us end this chapter, as we began, with a story. This is the reminiscence by Joseph Dov Soloveitchik, one of the leading Orthodox Jewish thinkers of the twentieth century, of his childhood in Central Europe:

> I recall, when I was young, I was a loner, afraid of the world . . . It seemed as if everyone made fun of me. But I had one friend – don't laugh – the Rambam [Maimonides]!

> The Rambam was a regular visitor to our home . . .

> Father's lectures were given in the hall of my grandfather's house, where my bed was placed. I used to sit on my bed and listen to Father's words, and he was always talking about the Rambam . . . He would open the *gemara* [Talmud], read through the section to be studied, and say . . . 'This is how it is explained by the Ri and the Tosafot; now let's look at the

Rambam and see how *he* explains it.' He would always discover that the Rambam explained it differently, and not in accordance with the obvious meaning. He would say . . . as if personally complaining to the Rambam: 'Rabbenu Moshe, why did you do this?' Everyone would be silent, so as not to disturb his thought. After a long time he would slowly raise his head, and begin: 'Gentlemen, let us see, now . . .'

I understood not a word of the subject, but two impressions fixed themselves in my innocent young brain: (1) The Rambam was surrounded by opponents and 'enemies' who wanted to harm him; (2) Father was his only defender. Who knows what would have happened to him without Father? . . .

I would go broken-hearted to my mother: 'Mother, Daddy can't explain the Rambam! What shall we do?' Mother would say, 'Father will find an answer for the Rambam. And if he can't, perhaps when you grow up you will find an answer for the Rambam. The main thing is to keep on learning Torah, and to enjoy it and let it excite you.' . . .

This was no golden daydream of a young child. It was a psychological and historical reality which even today lives in the depths of my soul. When I sit and learn I find myself at once in the company of the wise men of tradition, and our relationship is a personal one. The Rambam is on my right, Rabbenu Tam on the left, Rashi sits in front and explains, Rabbenu Tam fires questions, Rambam makes decisions, Raavad criticizes. All of them are in my little room . . . They look at me with affection, joining in reasoning and *gemara*, support and encourage me like a father.

The learning of Torah is not merely a didactic exercise . . . but the powerful expression of a love that crosses the generations, a marriage of spirits, a unity of souls. Those who hand down the Torah meet in one inn of history with those who receive it.

Chapter 6
Making a Jewish home

You are Jewish. You have just married, and you are about to set up your new home. What happens next?

Stop for a moment to think. You have saddled yourself with a mortgage and actually have a house or apartment of your own to live in. Lucky you! You are one of the fortunate few, if we look at Jewish populations world-wide, rather than at the minority who can afford to live in the more gracious suburbs of New York or London or Johannesburg. Plenty of Jews do not have a roof over their heads, or at best have to squeeze into a very small and none too private space made available to them in their parents' home.

Perhaps you do not care. If so, you are that ordinary enough person, the indifferent Jew. But for the purpose of this exercise let us assume that you are, if not a holy saint, a man or woman ready and willing to dedicate your life to the ideals of Torah. You will not be ordinary, but you will not be unique either.

Tzedaka

So, you are an idealist. Then the first thing that you will be looking at is what you can do to help those who do not share your good fortune. Most likely, at the wedding itself, you, or your parents, distributed alms to the needy; in your grandparents' days, especially if they lived in some East European *shtetl* (village), they would have invited the local poor to take part in the celebration and festive meals, but in 'civilized' city society this is not very practicable.

You have an income as well as a home. Then you must make proper allowance for *tzedaka* (charitable giving). One-tenth of your profits should be set aside for charitable purposes. This idea of the tithe comes from scripture; the Bible lays down that farmers in the land of Israel should set aside tithes of cattle, sheep, and produce, for priests and Levites (who were a public charge) and for the poor. As Asher ben Yehiel, a German who became Chief Rabbi of Barcelona (Spain) in the thirteenth century, reasoned, it would not make sense if we were to become better off by having been exiled from our Land on account of our sins; since today we do not give tithes of produce to priests and Levites we should at least give a tenth (some say a fifth) of our money profits to worthy causes and needy individuals.

The 'tenth' is a matter of conscience, not a tax levied by the community. Nor should it be taken too precisely. There are occasions when public need is such that you need to give more than a tenth; conversely, there are circumstances in which your immediate family's needs must be given priority. In any case, modern fiscal practice makes it hard to determine what a 'tenth of profit' is; is it before or after tax, or to what extent are the monies levied in taxation spent on projects which themselves count as *tzedaka* – education, housing, and health, for instance?

You, when you set up your home, will not worry about the finer points. What you will aim at is to ensure that your home is a base for a way of life guided by *tzedaka*. This will not be just the giving of money, but charity in the broadest human sense; hospitality to the learned, strangers, the needy, visiting the sick, general care and concern for the welfare of other people.

Mezuza

Now your conscience has been settled we can look at the house itself. The *Shema* (see p. 76) contains this phrase: 'And you shall write them [i.e. God's words] on the doorposts of your house and upon your gates'. As the rabbis interpret it, this means that the two sections of Deuteronomy containing the verse – that is, the first two paragraphs of the *Shema* – should be written in ink on parchment, placed in a container, and affixed to the door frame at least two-thirds of the way up (but not in the top span) on the right-hand side as you enter. The container, with its parchment, is called a *mezuza*, which just means 'doorpost'. You will see one on the front door of many Jewish houses, and on all except the bathroom doors in the houses of the more observant Orthodox Jews.

What you won't see without asking, because they are unlikely to be on display, are the *tallit* and *tefillin* worn by Orthodox men at certain services. The *tallit*, sometimes referred to as a 'prayer shawl', is a rectangular piece of material, preferably wool, with fringes at each of its four corners (in accordance with Num. 15: 37–41); it is draped around the shoulders at morning prayers. The *tefillin*, or 'prayer boxes' (the word 'phylacteries' is not a translation – it comes from the Greek for 'protectors'), are two leather boxes with straps attached; they contain the four biblical passages which include the instruction 'you shall bind them on your arms and they shall be an ornament between your eyes'; at the weekday morning service men (rarely, in Conservative and Reform congregations, women) bind one around the left arm opposite the heart, and the other on the forehead.

Other religious objects you might expect to find in a Jewish home include the Sabbath candlesticks, the eight-branched *menora*, or *hannukiya*, for the festival of Chanukah, and a spice box and candle-holder for the *havdala* ceremony performed at the end of Sabbaths and festivals. Then there will be, not necessarily on show, a variety of

10. *Tallit* and *tefillin*, worn at weekday morning service. On Sabbaths and Festivals the *tallit* is worn but not the *tefillin*.

goblets, and a special dish for the Passover Seder (see p. 60). Many of these objects will be skilled works of art, possibly prized family heirlooms.

Books and education

The phrase 'people of the Book' comes from the Quran, which uses it of both Jews and Christians, the people 'mentioned in the Book'. It does not mean 'people who read lots of books', but if it did it would still be an apt description of Jews. The library in your new home will certainly contain *siddurim* (prayer books), *mahzorim* (festival books), *haggadot (for the Passover feast), and chumashim* (copies of the Pentateuch, the first five books of the Bible, very likely with commentaries such as that of Rashi) which you acquired in school or as Bar- or Batmitzvah or even wedding presents.

If you are a little more learned you will have a set of twenty or so handsomely bound Hebrew volumes of Babylonian Talmud, as well as a selection of other Jewish classics. Israel is probably the only country in which the daily papers can compete against each other by offering free or reduced-price copies of the Babylonian Talmud to readers; if you live there you may have won your copy in a quiz or lottery.

This is the 'heavy' stuff, to which you will have added general Jewish books, of history or literature or humour, and records, tapes, CDs, and videos of your favourite Jewish entertainment, not to speak of your Internet connections to Jewish and Israeli sites, and your regular reading of the local Jewish newspaper – if in Britain, most likely the *Jewish Chronicle*, which describes itself as 'the world's leading Jewish newspaper, established 1841'.

The books will not remain as decorations on the shelf. You will invite the rabbi, or your friends, to come to your home regularly to take part in *shiurim*, or study sessions, on Talmud, or Bible, or some other traditional text, and this will be the high point of your week – or day, if you can manage a daily session.

As we saw in the last chapter, the learning of Torah is one of the highest spiritual values in Judaism. It is also a source of greatest joy in the home. Learning is not just for children, or for an élite, but for *all Israel*. One of the most encouraging developments on the otherwise highly conservative Orthodox scene in recent years has been the broadening of Torah learning programmes to include women, whose education has often in the past been neglected or even disapproved.

Kosher food

An increasing number of young Jews are becoming vegetarian, whether for health or economic reasons or out of consideration for the welfare of animals. Some seek support in scripture or tradition – Adam and Eve were vegetarians, and, according to the fifteenth-century rabbi, statesman, and Bible commentator Isaac Abravanel, we will all be vegetarians when the Messiah comes (his followers overlook his additional predictions that we will be anarchists and naturists and not live in houses).

But let us assume that you are setting up an omnivorous kitchen – at least, as omnivorous as is permitted by the 'laws of kashrut' – that is, the laws of Torah regulating kosher diet. (The word 'kosher', or 'kasher', just means 'OK'. Most Jews use the word *trefa* as its opposite.)

First of all, note which animals, birds, and fishes are permitted. Lists are in the Bible, in Leviticus chapter 11, some of which is repeated in Deuteronomy chapter 14. Only those animals having divided hooves and chewing the cud are permitted – in practice, cow, sheep, goat, and deer, but not pig, camel, horse, or rabbit. A list of forbidden birds is given, which implies that all others are permitted; since it is impossible to identify with certainty all those listed, the rabbis permit us to eat only birds known by tradition to be kosher, such as ducks, geese, pigeons, peacocks, and domestic fowl. All fish with scales and fins may be eaten; this excludes molluscs and crustaceans (octopus, shellfish, crab, etc.) and also eels, sharks, and some others not considered to have 'proper' scales. Certain types of locusts are permitted to those who have a tradition by which they can identify them.

Animals and birds, even of the permitted type, are not kosher unless slaughtered by the method known as *shechita*. The *shochet*, who must be licensed by a rabbi to perform *shechita*, uses a sharp knife to cut through the windpipe and oesophagus of the animal, at the same time severing the main arteries and causing virtually instantaneous loss of consciousness; if practised correctly, the method is as 'humane' as any. Additional blood is drained from the meat by a process of washing, salting, and rinsing, for centuries the prerogative of the housewife but nowadays mostly undertaken by the kosher butcher or supplier.

A strictly kosher household will have two sets of utensils for the preparation and consumption of food, one a 'meaty' set for use with meat and its derivatives, the other 'milky' for use with dairy and non-animal foods, since it is forbidden to mix milk and meat.

Not all Jews are equally strict in their observance of kashrut (what is or is not kosher). Some Reformers reject the system entirely, stressing that the essence of Judaism is ethics, not diet (in principle the Orthodox agree with this, but do not see it as a reason to abandon kashrut). Then there are those who won't eat pork, but will eat everything else, and those who will not eat any non-kosher meat but ignore other restrictions, or those who eat kosher at home but not when they are out, or those who would never eat non-kosher meat but do not seem to worry that bakery or confectionery may contain non-kosher fats or additives. A minority observe restrictions on wine and cheese, even when these do not contain non-kosher ingredients. At the far right of the spectrum are people who observe a host of additional 'precautionary' measures and are unlikely to accept any food other than that prepared under full rabbinic supervision.

Custom, family and social relations, and personal temperament will determine where any individual finds him- or herself on the kashrut spectrum. If inviting or being invited, it is best to be open and explicit about the rules you, your host, or your guest, follow; if in doubt, ask.

Sexual and personal relationships

Both the Bible and the Talmud allow polygamy, though by Talmudic times it was no longer common practice. In Western Europe, around 1000 CE, Rabbi Gershom of Mainz placed a ban of excommunication on any man who would take more than one wife, save in certain limited circumstances. The ban was quickly accepted by Jews in most Christian countries, though not in Islamic countries, where Talmud and Quran both counselled a limit of four wives per man, provided he could supply their sexual as well as their economic needs.

Sexual relations outside marriage are forbidden; it is not clear when the formal practice of concubinage ceased. The fact that something is forbidden does not mean it does not take place. 'Living together' is common in Jewish circles in Western countries, and there are, of course, Jewish adulterers and fornicators. The same discrepancy between traditional rules and contemporary practice exists with regard to sexual orientation and lifestyle. Biblical and rabbinic law unanimously condemn homosexual practices, but this has not prevented the formation of Jewish 'gay' clubs and even Synagogues.

For the law-abiding, however, there are restrictions on sexual activity even within marriage. Some restrictions are aimed at decency, or protection of an unwilling partner. The major restriction is that on sexual relations with a menstruant woman (*niddah*); the formal state of *niddah* remains for seven days after the menstrual flow has ceased, and until the woman has immersed herself totally in the *mikveh*, or ritual bath. Immersion in the *mikveh* is a sort of purification ceremony, also used by (amongst others) priests in the Temple before Divine Service, or by converts on adopting Judaism. 'Baptism' is simply the Greek translation of the Hebrew *tevila*, immersion.

The marriage relationship is one of mutual love, respect, and support. It is entered into on a permanent basis. Rabbinic Judaism, following the Hebrew scriptures, has always permitted divorce, though there has been much debate about the circumstances in which it is appropriate. Marriage, once entered into according to Jewish law, can be dissolved only by that law, which requires the handing over of a *get*, or bill of divorce, from husband to wife, in the presence of witnesses. Orthodox women have often suffered great hardship through this requirement, for little can be done to force a husband to authorize a *get* if he is unwilling, and the rabbinical courts will not simply 'dissolve' a marriage. Recently, steps have been taken to ameliorate the situation, taking advantage of a variety of legal processes available in different countries.

Most traditional communities emphasize the importance of family; after all, it is within the family that traditional values are most powerfully expressed and transmitted. Judaism is no exception, though Jewish families in the Western democracies have been subjected to the same disruptive pressures as families in other communities, and the family is no longer as strong as it was.

The downside of the emphasis on family values is the danger of marginalizing the stranger, the single, and the unattached. Deutero-Isaiah seems to have been well aware of this two and a half thousand years ago:

> The foreigner who has given his allegiance to the Lord must not say,
> 'The Lord will keep me separate from his people for ever';
>   and the eunuch must not say,

11. Wedding customs vary widely, with each community anxious to preserve its own traditions. Here a member of the Inbal Dance Theatre, Israel, dresses as a Yemenite Jewish bride.

'I am nothing but a barren tree.'

For these are the words of the Lord:

The eunuchs who keep my sabbaths,

who choose to do my will and hold fast to my covenant,

shall receive from me something better than sons and daughters,

a memorial and a name in my own house and within my walls;

I will give them an everlasting name,

a name imperishable for all time.

(Isa. 56: 2–5, *New English Bible*)

Many Jewish communities have a long way to go before the stranger, the single, and the unattached feel as comfortable within them as Isaiah would have liked.

Life cycle

Judaism

Shakespeare spoke of 'seven ages' of man – the infant, 'mewling and puking in his nurse's arms', the whining schoolboy, the lover, the soldier, the justice, the sixth age which 'shifts | Into the lean and slipper'd pantaloon', and, finally, 'second childishness, and mere oblivion' (*As You Like It*, II. vii. 139–66).

Jewish sociologists now identify seven life stages marked by rites of passage. The seven are not Shakespearian, nor do they correspond exactly to the stages of life noted by Jewish tradition, but they will serve our purposes.

1. Birth

Males – circumcision on the eighth day – feast – ancient tradition going back to the days of Abraham.

Male firstborn – additional 'Redemption' ceremony at 30 days.

Females – no traditional ceremony, but (*a*) mother attends the synagogue for thanksgiving prayer, and/or (*b*), especially in Reform synagogues, baby is brought into the synagogue for blessing.

2. Growing up

Optional and varied ceremonies take place as a child starts to learn the Hebrew alphabet – eating letters made of honey cake etc.

Boys celebrate Barmitzvah at 13. This is an individual ceremony, at which the boy reads Torah in the Synagogue, has a great party, and receives presents.

Girls may celebrate Batmitzvah at 12 – a Reform ceremony similar to that for boys. Orthodox Jews have only recently started to mark Batmitzvah publicly, usually with a collective ceremony for girls of the year group, plus individual parties. Many Orthodox prefer 'Bat Chayil' to Batmitzvah ceremonies; like confirmation, Bat Chayil normally takes place at a later age, and only when a prescribed course of study has been satisfactorily completed.

Liberal and Reform synagogues have abandoned their erstwhile preference for confirmation over Bar- and Batmitzvah.

3. Marriage

From the point of view of Jewish law, a wedding consists of two distinct procedures. First there is *kiddushin* (betrothal). In the presence of witnesses, the groom gives an object (nowadays a wedding ring) to the bride, and says 'You are betrothed to me by means of this ring in accordance with the law of Moses and Israel'; the bride need say nothing, for her silence is taken as acquiescence. Two blessings are then recited, and a cup of wine shared.

Then comes *nisuin*, or marriage proper. The bride and groom stand beneath the Chuppa (bridal canopy), symbolizing their new home, and seven blessings are recited, a cup of wine again being shared. The couple are blessed, and the groom smashes a glass, recalling the destruction of Jerusalem even on his most joyful day. Then, in the presence of witnesses, bride and groom are secluded for a time.

A wedding may be plain and simple, or it may be choral and floral, with bridal gowns and morning suits and parents leading the couple to the Chuppa and speeches and congratulations and singing and dancing and feasting – feasting, indeed, for seven days and seven nights. *Hasidim* and right-of-centre Orthodox separate the sexes throughout.

Reform Jews equalize the roles of bride and groom, have an exchange of rings and perhaps promises, dispense with the seclusion, and feast only at the wedding itself, not on successive nights.

The variety of customs amongst Orthodox and Reform, occidental and oriental Jews is vast. Music ranges from ball-room to Klezmer, from pop to classics; people have even been known to entertain with a consort of viols, but this is too quiet for most tastes.

4. Parenthood

The art of bringing up children was not mastered by Moses, King David, or the philosopher Plato. Professional training for well-meaning parents is available at Synagogue Community Centres. Children are resilient, however, and grow up despite the training.

5. Mid-life

Only recently, with increased life-expectancy, have sociologists begun to categorize mid-life and its crises as a distinct stage of human development – or disintegration. Appropriate rites of passage have yet to be devised.

6. Old age

The ideal is to have achieved wisdom through life's experiences, and to be the focus of admiration and respect from those immature beings still battling through the previous stages. It applies to women as much as to men. Sometimes it happens. Often, however, the reality is uncomfortably more akin to Shakespeare's 'second childishness, and mere oblivion, | Sans teeth, sans eyes, sans taste, sans everything'.

7. Death

Orthodox Jews have burial only; Reform Jews may have cremation or burial.

The close relatives (spouse, parents, siblings, children) rend an outer garment, remove their shoes, and 'sit *shiva*' – that is, they sit on the ground or on low stools at home, where friends come to visit and comfort them and prayers are said daily. Though *shiva* means 'seven', denoting seven days of mourning, the less observant make do with one night only. Others attend to the mourners' material needs, such as preparing their meals.

A further period of less intensive mourning continues for the remainder of thirty days, and children mourn twelve months for parents. After that, there is an annual remembrance day, or *Jahrzeit*. The closest relative recites *kaddish* (not a memorial prayer, but a doxology) in the synagogue for the first eleven months and annually on the *Jahrzeit*.

Belief in life after death has been endorsed by Reform as well as Orthodox theologians. In the past there was debate as to whether life after death involved some form of bodily resurrection, or only the perdurance of the 'soul'; the debate continues, and nowadays has broadened to include those who regard talk about life after death as a metaphor for continuing repute or influence.

Chapter 7
Out of the ghetto, into the whirlwind

In previous chapters we have come across different denominations (they do not like to be called 'sects') of Jews, such as Orthodox and Reform. Why should such divisions exist? How did they come about? Is there not one 'pure, authentic' Judaism, which Moses brought down the mountain all those millennia ago? To answer these questions we have to go back a little in time.

Unfortunately we cannot go back to some 'pure, authentic Torah' received and handed on by Moses. Jewish tradition and Christian tradition both believe there was one, and Jewish tradition believes that it was preserved by the rabbis. Ultimately, this is matter of faith. No one can establish the text of such a Torah, and historians cannot tell us of a time when one monolithic Judaism was accepted unquestioningly by all Jews as authentic. As we saw in Chapter 2, when we enquired how Judaism and Christianity split apart, even in the first century several forms of Judaism existed side by side, and each lay claim to being the authentic Torah. Christianity, in its turn, made a similar claim, that Jesus was the 'fulfilment' of Torah, and that Christians were the 'true Israel'.

What about the Middle Ages, the 'Age of Faith', when everybody shared the same beliefs and followed the same rules? Such a view of the Middle Ages is naïve. Medieval society was authoritarian and oppressive; if you entertained views different from those of the authorities, you kept quiet about it. If you could not keep quiet, you were at least careful; you disguised your opinions in mystical language or appealed to a 'true, hidden tradition' such as the 'Hermetic Tradition'. Beneath the surface there was far more questioning than is commonly assumed. Though the only Jewish sect that established itself and flourished in the Middle Ages was that of the Karaites (the Karaites, needless to say, regard 'Rabbanite' Judaism as the 'sect' and their own religion as the true, original Judaism), we can now discern, with hindsight, traces of many of the dissidents who failed to gain a hearing.

In Western Christendom the Church of Rome exercised spiritual domination and was not reluctant to use the 'secular arm' – that is, the civil authorities and their armies – to ensure conformity in doctrine and practice. The Church defined 'heresy', and repressed it severely, as when Pope Innocent III launched the armed Crusade that brutally repressed the Albigenses and desolated much of southern France.

The Jews had no pope and no armies, nor, with very few exceptions, did they ever have recourse to the cruel physical punishments and tortures that were routine in the surrounding world. But they were no less vigilant in confronting what they regarded as heresy. The communal leaders exercised power not through physical repression but through the *herem* – a thirty-day renewable ban of excommunication, used to secure compliance with civil and criminal justice as well as religious law. Excommunication carried grave consequences for social and economic life, for an excommunicated Jew was cut off from his community and did not belong anywhere else; there was no way for him to earn a living, no place for him in society.

This system of communal discipline (or oppression) collapsed with the walls of the ghetto. In the eighteenth century, when a significant number of Jews in some Western countries began to acquire civil rights, the traditional elders and rabbis lost control over the way of life of the Jewish masses. Questions and dissident opinions could no longer be suppressed. Jews quickly seized on Enlightenment ideas of civil liberty, toleration, and individualism, and on the fashionable contempt for 'superstition'. Many of them started to perceive the traditional Jewish community and its institutions as obscurantist, out-of-date, superstitious.

Moses Mendelssohn (see p. 51), who remained an observant Jew throughout his life, radically reinterpreted Judaism to conform with an Enlightenment outlook. Many, including Mendelssohn's own children – his grandson, the famous composer Felix Mendelssohn, was born to baptized parents – accepted baptism, not because they were convinced of the truth or superiority of the Christian religion but rather, as another baptized Jew, the poet Heinrich Heine, put it, because it was a ticket to 'civilization' and cultured society.

By the end of the eighteenth century three options remained to West European Jews, particularly in Germany and France. They could assimilate – which in practice meant baptism and the loss of Jewishness. They could retrench, maintain their traditions unmodified, and turn their backs on Enlightenment, though at the expense of social alienation and ridicule and quite possibly the loss of hard-gained civil rights. The remaining possibility was to change, to 'modernize' Judaism by cleansing it of superstitious and outmoded elements (Christians, after all, were attempting to accomplish the same with their own religion), and hence to gain social acceptance without abandoning Jewish identity. Reform emerged from this third option. It was not, at first, intended to be a separate movement. Only when the proposed changes were rejected by the traditionalists was Reform, as a distinct movement, born, and only then was the label 'Orthodox' firmly attached to those who opposed radical change.

Reform Judaism

The early nineteenth-century German Reformers sought to regenerate public worship by enhancing its beauty and relevance, cutting obsolete material, introducing vernacular prayers, a weekly vernacular sermon, choral and organ music, and new ceremonies such as confirmation. The French occupation of Westphalia created the opportunity for Israel Jacobson to erect the first Reform Temple based on these principles at Seesen in 1810, but the French withdrawal ended the experiment. In Berlin Orthodox opposition limited Reform to a weekly service in Jacobson's own home. The first lasting Reform Temple was therefore that of Hamburg, erected in 1818.

The controversy engendered by vociferous Orthodox opposition to Reform in Hamburg soon brought to the surface the theological issues that underlay the differences in attitude to liturgical reform. Principal amongst these issues was the authority of the Talmud and rabbinic interpretation. The Reformers tried at first to justify themselves by an appeal to traditional authority, but it soon became evident that they did not regard themselves as bound by traditional norms and formulations of Judaism. They had, for instance, abandoned prayers for the coming of a personal Messiah, and were adopting the critical historical method of reading Jewish texts, including the Bible.

Out of the struggle to resolve such issues grew the theological concept of Progressive Revelation. Perhaps, as Spinoza had argued, the old biblical laws (not to speak of rabbinic law) were the law of the ancient Hebrew polity, and were no longer applicable in a modern society in which new ethical, moral, and spiritual values were 'revealed'. Christianity had by no means superseded Judaism; Judaism itself, rightly interpreted, had always been a religion of spirituality and could even now demonstrate the progress of revelation. This Reform understanding was strengthened as the nineteenth century adopted progress and evolution as its watch-words.

Reform spread rapidly throughout Germany and beyond to Austria, Hungary, France, and Denmark, as well as to Britain, where on 27 January 1842 the West London Synagogue, today a thriving Reform centre, was dedicated, though the founders of the West London Synagogue had no clear intention of setting up a distinct Reform movement. In the USA, a Reformed Society of Israelites had been set up in Charleston, South Carolina, in 1824; it not only called for liturgical revisions, but adopted the Thirteen Principles of the Faith of Maimonides (see Appendix A), excluding the articles on the coming of the Messiah and bodily resurrection (cynics have compared this to formally accepting the Ten Commandments, excluding two which appear to be inconvenient). Later in the century, under Isaac M. Wise's leadership, Reform became a strong force in American Jewry. Hebrew Union College was founded at Cincinnati in 1875, where it remains to this day as the spiritual home of Reform. The classical formulations of Reform, the 'Platforms' of Philadelphia 1869 (see the full text in Appendix B on p. 137) and Pittsburg 1885, were likewise American achievements.

As the nineteenth century drew to a close the Reform premiss that society and culture would approach ever more closely the universalist ideals of the Enlightenment, that all humankind, Jews included, would experience continued 'messianic' progress, came to appear out of touch with reality. Not only had a new, secular racial anti-Semitism taken root, but even liberal Christian theologians persisted in contrasting Gospel with Law, New Testament with Old, spirituality with legality, in a way which upheld the view of Christianity as having superseded Judaism. The Reform response to this was to stress even more strongly the ethical and spiritual dimension of Judaism, a position clearly articulated by Hermann Cohen. Proclaiming Judaism as 'ethical monotheism', Cohen developed the messianic idea as a constant response to the divine, a call to the never-ending task of moral improvement; messianism enabled an ongoing critique of society. In his later work he regained a sense of the significance of the

Sabbath and other religious institutions, and of the specific vocation of Israel.

Because of its emphasis on universalism and on acculturation within the 'host' societies, Reform was unsympathetic, even hostile, towards the Zionist movement. Even before the establishment of the State of Israel, however, attitudes were changing, as universalist ideals in 'enlightened' Europe were eroded by nationalist conflict, persistent anti-Semitism, and the rise of Fascism in Germany and elsewhere. The Columbus Platform of 1937 shows a broader balance than early Reform pronouncements between the universalist and particularist aspects of Judaism and a commitment to the 'rehabilitation of Palestine'.

The San Francisco Platform of 1976 reflects the impact of the Holocaust and of the establishment of the State of Israel; there is less faith in human progress, less clarity on God, a greater appreciation of home life and ritual and of the place of Israel in Jewish life, and a sense of the 'covenant theology' then being worked out in Reform circles.

Liturgy has always been a central concern for Reformers. Recent prayer books are deeply influenced by reflection on the Holocaust, the State of Israel, and the need to develop 'inclusivist' language. Hebrew has regained prominence, and modern psychology and anthropology have restored appreciation of ritual and ethnicity.

There was no partition in front of the women in the Hamburg Temple of 1818, and many of the liturgical reforms were for their benefit; nevertheless, they were seated separately on a balcony and could not be called to the reading of the Torah. In the twentieth century considerable progress was made towards the equalization of women's status. The first woman actually to receive ordination within the movement – and therefore the first ever woman rabbi – was Regina Jonas, who served briefly as a rabbi before perishing in the Holocaust; she was ordained by Rabbi Max Dienemann on behalf of the Union of Liberal Rabbis in

12. American Reform Jews refer to the Synagogue as 'Temple', and have experimented with modern architectural styles. Temple Beth Shalom, at Elkins Park, Philadelphia, was designed by Frank Lloyd Wright and built in 1954.

Germany on 27 December 1935. Though the Central Conference of American Rabbis, following the lead of some Protestant denominations, endorsed the principle of ordaining women in the late 1950s, it was not until 1972 that a female rabbi, Sally Priesand, received ordination from the Hebrew Union College in Cincinnati.

Reform, especially in the USA, has introduced changes to traditional Jewish law regarding personal status. Many Reform rabbis have been prepared to officiate at mixed marriages – that is, marriages where only one partner is Jewish. In 1983 the Central Conference of American Rabbis (Reform) declared a child should be regarded as Jewish if either parent was Jewish, rather than only if the mother was, as is the norm in traditional Judaism; this change was made in an attempt to equalize the status of the sexes; the Liberal movement in the UK takes the same line as the CCAR. In the 1990s there has been much debate in Reform circles on attitudes to 'alternative lifestyles'; some have sanctioned 'marriages' between persons of the same sex.

Reform Judaism accounts for about 35 per cent of US and 15 per cent of British Synagogue allegiance, with smaller percentages in other countries, including those of the former Soviet Union. Active in Israel, it lacks formal recognition; its marriages and conversions are not fully recognized by the state.

'Liberal' and 'Reform' are used interchangeably in most places, but in Britain 'Liberal' denotes the movement created around 1909 by Lily Montagu and Claude Montefiore, and which is distinguished from Reform by a more radical approach to tradition and ritual, British Reform being closer to a Conservative position.

Orthodox Judaism

The term 'orthodox', first used in 1807, was adopted by the German Reformers as a label for their traditionalist opponents. But it cannot be defined, other than to say that it is an umbrella term for all those forms of traditional Judaism which were left behind when first Reform, then Conservative Judaism, set up as organizations dedicated to specific programmes in some way critical of traditional Judaism as commonly interpreted.

Certainly, contemporary Orthodoxy comprises many and varied trends. It includes, for instance, a large variety of Hasidic sects, though Hasidism itself was regard as deviant and 'reformist' at its time of origin. Orthodoxy also includes the *mitnagdim*, or opponents of Hasidism, whose Judaism is found at its most profound and influential in the Lithuanian-style *yeshivot* (talmudic colleges), which highlight the value of intensive study of the *halakhic* (legal) texts of the Talmud and other rabbinic literature.

Yet a further element comes from 'modern' or 'centrist' Orthodoxy, which attempts a practical synthesis between tradition and general culture, following the German rabbi Samson Raphael Hirsch (1808–88), who endorsed the concept of 'Torah with the way of the land'. And the *Musar* movement of Israel Salanter (1810–83) has contributed a distinctive emphasis on personal ethical and spiritual discipline, embodied in the person of the *mashgiah ruhani*, or Dean, of the *yeshiva*, whose task it is to inspire the students to self-criticism and spiritual growth.

Then there are the various 'regional' flavours which have shaped the practice of Judaism without modifying its structures in any radical way. Ashkenazi ('German' – that is, North European) and Sephardi ('Spanish' – that is, South European, North African, and Middle Eastern) Jewry have their distinctive customs, often rooted in local culture, which impart diversity to contemporary Orthodoxy. There has occasionally been social friction between them; in Israel, for instance, Sephardi leaders have sometimes complained that Ashkenazim have privileged access to government office. Such disputes are cultural rather than religious.

Despite all this diversity, Orthodox leaders have attempted to define Orthodoxy, or what they prefer to call 'authentic' or 'Torah-true' Judaism. One way is to stress that Orthodox Jews regard *halakha* (Jewish law) as binding. The other way is to stress belief in *Torah min ha-Shamayim*, the divine revelation of Torah at Sinai, as the distinctive feature of Orthodoxy. This is very problematic. First of all, to define Judaism in terms of dogma is itself a departure from tradition, even though there is precedent for it, for instance in the works of Maimonides. But unfortunately the doctrine is in need of reinterpretation in the light of modern scholarship. If understood in its naïve medieval form, it would be rejected by a large proportion of those who call themselves Orthodox; but if it is to be understood in some other way, many non-Orthodox Jews would claim that they believe in it, too.

So it may be wiser not to attempt to define Orthodoxy, but simply to list organizations which regard themselves as Orthodox, and to note that individual members of those organizations may interpret their allegiance with great flexibility.

In Israel Orthodoxy is the only officially recognized form of Judaism, allowing its rabbis the monopoly of marriage regulation and determination of status for Jews, though some headway has recently been made in acknowledging non-Orthodox marriages. Worldwide, outside North America, the vast majority of religiously affiliated Jews are nominally Orthodox, even though at the personal level their beliefs or practices may be closer to those of Reform.

Notwithstanding the activities and influence of the Israel Chief Rabbinate, the Conference of European Rabbis, the Rabbinical Council of America, and similar bodies, there is no overall direction in Orthodoxy. Decisions in *halakha* are strongly influenced by independent 'Torah sages' recognized for their learning and piety. Decisions range from ritual matters to the conduct of war and peace, from medical ethics and civil disputes to the status of women; the presumption is that the laws of Torah are of divine origin and eternally valid, to be interpreted in each generation by its Torah sages (see Chapter 9 for examples).

Conservative Judaism

If the German Zacharias Frankel (1801–75) was the ideological father of Conservative Judaism, Solomon Schechter (1850–1915), at the Jewish Theological Seminary of America, forged the movement. Conservative Jews accord a central position to *halakha*, but are readier than the Orthodox to modify its provisions in the light of changing social and economic circumstances, insisting that Judaism in its most vital periods has retained its essential ethos whilst interacting positively with the surrounding culture. They accept the findings of modern historical criticism with regard to the composition of biblical and other source documents.

When a majority voted in 1983 that women might be ordained, several leading rabbis felt that that violated the limits of *halakha*; they eventually broke away, forming the Union for Traditional Judaism.

Conservative Judaism is particularly strong in the USA, where it is possibly the largest single Jewish denomination. In Israel and the UK, where it is known by its Hebrew name 'Masorti', it is a more recent development, but it has attracted numerous adherents. It has made inroads elsewhere, though only in North America does it approach one third of synagogue allegiance.

Reconstructionist Judaism

Based on the philosophy of Mordecai M. Kaplan (1881–1983), powered by the Reconstructionist Rabbinical College founded in 1968, Reconstructionists call for a reappraisal of Judaism, including such fundamental concepts as God, Israel, and Torah, and institutions such as the Synagogue, in the light of contemporary thought and society. Reconstructionists work through the participatory *chavura*, in which the rabbi is a resource person rather than a leader, and decisions are reached by consensus. From the inception of the movement women have been granted equal status, and since 1968 persons with either parent Jewish have been accepted as Jewish. Though organized groups beyond the USA and Israel are few, Reconstructionist thought has powerfully influenced other trends.

Chapter 8
Twentieth-century Judaism

No religion has emerged unscathed from the twentieth century. New scientific discoveries and historical criticism have kept alive questions raised since early modern times about the truth and 'authenticity' of sacred texts. Increasing secularization of government in the West has undermined the power of the religious leadership. People's values have changed. The pursuit of equal and universal human rights, irrespective of race, colour, gender, or creed, is seen as important; the pursuit of correct doctrine is perceived as neither important nor achievable. Individual freedom to go your own way, even in sexual matters, provided you do not harm anyone else, is taken for granted.

Large numbers of men and women have abandoned organized religion, some because they have found it intellectually untenable, more because they have found it emotionally unsatisfying, most because they have found that its demands inhibit the personal freedom which they regard as a fundamental human right.

If Western Christianity has been most strongly affected, Western Judaism runs it a close second, for both have their home in the lands in which modernity and the Enlightenment were nurtured.

At the same time, religion has shown greater persistence and resilience than the humanists of a century ago believed that it would. Even in the

Soviet Union, seventy years of atheist propaganda and scorn for religion failed to eradicate religious sentiment. In the Jewish world, the demise of Hasidism was widely assumed, in the first half of the twentieth century, to be imminent, and to be speedily followed by the collapse of other forms of Orthodoxy, yet in the latter half of the century Hasidism experienced a revival, and even made considerable inroads into other Orthodox communities, and the *baal teshuva* movement, of 'reborn' Jews finding their religious roots, gained considerable momentum.

Judaism has been subjected to the same pressures, intellectual, social, and moral, as other religions, and has responded in similar ways. Yet world Jewry has found itself at the centre of two twentieth-century events which have affected it in unique ways. One of these is the trauma of the Shoah, or Holocaust – the systematic humiliation and genocide in the years 1933–44 of about six million Jews in Central Europe. The other is the establishment of the State of Israel.

In this chapter we will take a brief look at four areas in which Jewish thought has developed in the twentieth century.

Zionism, religion, and the State of Israel

Zionism – the idea of the return of the people Israel to the land of Israel – is clearly rooted in the Bible, where prophet after prophet assures the exiles in Babylon that they will be restored to their land. David Ben Gurion, who in 1948 became the first prime minister of the new state, declared in his testimony before the Peel Commission in 1937, when Britain held the League of Nations' Mandate for Palestine: 'It is not the mandate which is our Bible, but the Bible which is our mandate.'

Ben Gurion, for all his love of the Bible, was a secular Zionist (see above). Jewish theologians have been ambivalent in their commitment to modern political Zionism. Some, such as Rav Kook (Abraham Isaac Kook, 1865–1935, first Chief Rabbi of Palestine in modern times), have

Israel/Palestine

Political History since the fall of Jerusalem to the Romans in 70 CE.

The Bible defines boundaries for the Land of Israel on both sides of the Jordan, but it is not possible to identify the whole boundary with certainty. The name 'Palestine', also, has been applied to areas on both sides of the river. Modern Israel comprises about one ninth of the biblical land; Jordan, the 'occupied territories' (now under Palestinian self-rule), and parts of Lebanon and Syria account for the rest.

70–395	Direct Roman rule
c.395–638	Byzantine rule
614–627	Jewish rule under Persians
c.638–1072	Arab rule
1072–1099	Seljuq rule
1099–1291	Crusader rule (intermittent)
1291–1516	Mameluke rule
1517–1917	Ottoman Turkish rule
1920(22)–1948	British rule, under mandate from the League of Nations
29 November 1947	United Nations resolves that there should be partition of Palestine into independent but economically linked Jewish and Arab states with Jerusalem under an international regime. Partition accepted by Jews but rejected by Arabs.
14 May 1948	Proclamation of Independence of the State of Israel
15 May 1948	British mandate terminates, and five Arab armies invade Israel, initiating Israel's 'War of Independence'.

1956	Suez War
1967	Six Day War, provoked by Egyptian blockade of Israeli access to Red Sea. Israel defeats several Arab armies, reunites Jerusalem, and occupies Sinai, West Bank, Gaza, and Golan (Syria).
1969–70	'War of Attrition' against Israel
October 1973	The fifth ('Yom Kippur') Arab–Israeli War
26 March 1979	Egypt–Israel Peace Treaty signed in Washington
April 1982	Sinai formally returned to Egypt
June 1982	Israel launches war against PLO bases in Lebanon, and eventually establishes 'security zone' in Southern Lebanon
December 1987	Palestinian 'Intifada' (uprising) commences against Israeli rule in West Bank and Gaza.
1993	Agreement between Israel and the Palestinians signed in Oslo, paving the way for Palestinian self-rule
October 1994	Peace Agreement between Israel and Jordan
October 1995	Interim Accord ('Oslo II') between Israel and the Palestinians signed.

been amongst its main architects; they see modern Israel as the fulfilment, or at least the beginning of fulfilment, of biblical prophecy. Others, such as the *Hasidim* of Sotmar, say that only a state set up under the Messiah and governed in accordance with 'true' Torah could be the fulfilment of prophecy; modern Israel does not meet that criterion.

Many Jews, including secular ones, see Israel as the fulfilment of the 'national' aspirations of the Jewish people; after thousands of years of minority status, of being alienated from the host societies, and in many cases actually prevented from becoming full citizens of the lands in which they lived, they feel that they have at last 'come home' and are able to control their own destiny within the normal limitations of independent statehood. Israel is perceived as a secure haven for persecuted Jews; had Israel existed during the years of the Holocaust, Jews would have had somewhere to turn to. Moreover, Israel provides the opportunity to live a fulfilling Jewish life free from the inhibitions and restrictions of minority status.

The status quo

Israel's legal system is basically a secular creation, inherited from the British Mandate period. Israel has no written constitution, and relations between State and 'Church' are based on a status quo which has four components:

1. The Jewish Sabbath and festivals are the national public holidays.
2. Kosher food is the standard for public institutions.
3. Personal status (marriage, divorce, and some aspects of inheritance) is subject to the jurisdiction of the rabbinical courts. (For non-Jews, personal status is governed by their own religious courts or tribunals.)
4. State schools belong either to the National Secular stream or to the National Religious stream. (Again, other religious communities have their own institutions.)

A bill enacted by the Knesset on 23 July 1980 states: 'Where a court finds that a question requiring a decision cannot be answered by reference to an enactment or a judicial precedent or by way of analogy, it shall decide the case in the light of the principles of freedom, justice, equity and peace of the heritage of Israel.'

Since Jews lacked political independence and power for almost 2,000 years, including the whole formative period of rabbinic Judaism, theologians have had to seek answers to a host of problems in 'Church–State' relationships which did not arise in practical form earlier.

There are many lively debates in contemporary Israel.

How far is it right to go in urging public compliance with religious standards? At what stage does the law of a democratically elected legislature cross the boundary into religious coercion?

Should marriages continue to be regulated by the religious courts, or should there be secular registration of marriages?

What are the implications of equal treatment before the law for religious minorities including 'dissidents' of one's own faith? In particular, why do Reform and Conservative rabbis not have the right to perform marriages equally with Orthodox rabbis, or, for that matter, with Christian and Muslim religious officials?

What should be done about issues such as abortion, medical experimentation, and autopsies, on which traditional Jewish law places severe restrictions?

How should external relations with countries of other faiths be conducted?

Is there such a thing as a 'just war', and if so, what are the conditions of engagement? Out of this debate emerged the novel concept of *tohar ha-nesheq* ('purity of arms'), which demands *inter alia* that the fighting force take special risks to avoid harm to non-combatants and to minimize enemy casualties.

In what form and under what circumstances should one supply either arms or alms to other nations?

Are all Jews obliged to live in the Land of Israel?

Israelis read the Bible and rabbinic literature as part of the history of their people, even if they are not personally religious. The common heritage of secular and religious Israelis heightens rather than diminishes the acrimony of debate, for the secular and the religious read that heritage in very different ways. Cynics remark that, if it were not for the cooperation demanded for military defence, the country would tear itself apart in controversy between the religious and the secular; undoubtedly the tensions are great.

Holocaust theology

Holocaust theology as a genre developed in the 1970s, but the foundation of Jewish attitudes to evil and suffering lies in scripture and has been a constant theme in Jewish theology.

The principle of *Kiddush Hashem* (sanctification of God's name) lays down that a Jew must be prepared to sacrifice his life rather than collaborate in murder, sexual immorality, or idolatry. Remarkably, many Jews, even under the extreme pressures of the Shoah, succeeded in maintaining a high standard of moral integrity, and, in accordance with the *halakha* (religious law), refusing all collaboration with their oppressors. They gave witness to God and their faith. Others were less steadfast; all were victims, not all were martyrs.

Rabbi Ephraim Oshry survived the Holocaust in the ghetto of Kovno, Lithuania. There, people approached him with their questions. He committed the questions and answers to writing on paper torn surreptitiously from cement sacks, and hid the writing in cans which he retrieved after the war: 'The daily life of the ghetto, the food we ate, the

13. These Jews may have been told they were going to a 'holiday camp'; in fact they were on their way to the largest and most ruthlessly efficient Death Factory in history. Estimates of the number who perished in Auschwitz range from two to four million. About 200,000 were non-Jews, including many Polish intellectuals and patriots; the remainder were Jews.

crowded quarters we shared, the rags on our feet, the lice in our skin, the relationships between men and women – all this was contained within the specifics of the questions . . .'

Amongst his titles are: 'Jews Forced to Shred a Torah Scroll', 'Sabbath Torah Reading for Slave Laborers', 'The Blessing for Martyrdom', 'Saving Oneself with a Baptismal Certificate', 'Contraceptives in the Ghetto', 'The Repentant Kapo'. Here is one short question and answer to illustrate how the traditional process of *halakha* gave sacred meaning to the lives and deaths of the victims.

'We Jews of the ghetto of Kovno . . . were enslaved by the Germans; were worked to the bone night and day without rest; were starved and were paid nothing. The German enemy decreed our total annihilation. We were completely dispensable. Most would die.' So was it proper to recite the customary blessing in the morning prayers thanking God 'who has not made me a slave'?

Oshry replied: 'One of the earliest commentators on the prayers points out that this blessing was not formulated in order to praise God for our physical liberty but rather for our spiritual liberty. I therefore ruled that we might not skip or alter this blessing under any circumstances. On the contrary, despite our physical captivity, we were more obligated than ever to recite the blessing to show our enemies that as a people we were spiritually free.'

Traditional explanations of suffering depend for their cogency not only on a strong sense of guilt, but also on the belief in life after death. This belief, whether expressed as bodily resurrection, eternal life of the spirit, or some combination, remains central in orthodox teaching. Some Jews, perhaps influenced by kabbala, have adopted the concept of reincarnation to explain the suffering of the apparently innocent, such as children.

Some regard the Holocaust as an act of God's righteous judgement on

Facts of the Holocaust

Many people prefer to use the Hebrew term *Shoah* (destruction) to denote the Nazi attempt to exterminate the Jews, since it is less theologically 'loaded' than 'Holocaust'.

Immediately on coming to power in 1933 Hitler began to enact the anti-Jewish legislation he had promised; anybody with one or more Jewish grandparent was defined as racially Jewish. Books by Jewish authors were burned, Jewish businesses boycotted, Jews excluded from the professions; the 1935 Nuremberg Laws consolidated this legislation and extended it to Austria and Czechoslovakia. On Kristallnacht, 9–10 November 1938, synagogues were burnt down, Jewish businesses looted, and thousands of Jews were sent to concentration camps.

Following the invasion of Poland Jews were herded into ghettos where many were murdered and others died from the appalling conditions.

At Wannsee (Berlin) in 1942 the decision was taken to implement the *Endlösung* ('Final Solution'), that is physically to exterminate all Jews. Extermination camps were established at Auschwitz, Belsen and elsewhere in Central Europe and Jews transported to them in inhuman conditions to be killed, generally by gassing followed by mass cremation; able-bodied Jews were subjected to forced labour under slave conditions before being killed. A systematic policy of humiliation and degradation was practised prior to the actual killing. In all, about six million Jews perished, perhaps two thirds of the Jewish population of Europe and one third of the world Jewish population.

Others perished also; but only the Jews, and perhaps some Gypsy groups, were singled out for total annihilation purely on account of 'race'.

the faithlessness of Israel to the covenant of Torah exemplified by apostasy, assimilation, and Reform; most Jews regard such remarks as insulting to both the dead and the survivors.

'It is clear beyond all doubt that the blessed Holy One is the ruler of the universe, and we must accept the judgement with love . . .' These words of the Hungarian Rabbi Shmuel David Ungar exactly express the simple faith of those who entered the gas chambers with *Ani Ma'amin* (the declaration of faith as formulated by Maimonides) or *Shema Israel* (Deut. 6: 4–9, declaring God's unity and the duty to love Him and obey His commandments) on their lips. What was happening defied their understanding, but their faith triumphed over evil and they were ready, in the traditional phrase, to 'sanctify the name of God' – *Kiddush Hashem*. God's love was proclaimed even in the depths of destruction.

The sense of the apocalyptic, of being part of the events heralding the Messiah and the final Redemption, was strong amongst the orthodox victims of the Shoah, and has become stronger since. Religious Zionists interpreted the Shoah and the strife surrounding the emergence of the State of Israel as 'birth pangs of the Messiah'.

The idea of God being 'hidden' features strongly, perhaps because of its full development by the mystics (kabbalists). It links with the midrashic idea of God, or rather the *Shekhina*, being 'in exile' with Israel, for 'I am with him in his distress' (Ps. 91: 15).

Elie Wiesel is perhaps the best known and most easily approachable writer on the Shoah. His stories are a 'narrative exegesis' of the Shoah. In the story *Night* the poignant question 'Where is God?' is answered by pointing to a Jewish child hanging on a gallows; suffering is seen to lead to salvation. In his play *The Trial*, a great anger against God is expressed; God himself is put on trial, yet at the end, when He is pronounced guilty, the 'judges' arise and say 'let us now pray'.

Richard Rubenstein was driven by reflection on the Shoah to reject the traditional idea of God as the 'Lord of history'. God simply failed to intervene to save his faithful. Though denying atheism, he urges both Christians and Jews to adopt non-theistic forms of religion, based on pagan or Asian models, and finds deep spiritual resources within the symbolism of Temple sacrifice.

Emil Fackenheim grounds his theology in the actual resistance of Shoah victims to whom no realistic hope remained: 'A philosophical Tikkun ['repair', 'restoration'] is possible after the Holocaust because a philosophical Tikkun already took place, however fragmentarily, during the Holocaust itself'; the rebirth of Israel, and a new constructive dialogue with a self-critical Christianity, are essential to this process. Fackenheim is also noted for his statement that there should be a 614th commandment, surplus to the 613 of tradition – to survive as Jews, to remember, never to despair of God, lest we hand Hitler a posthumous victory.

J. D. Soloveitchik was more poetic, and more traditional in his understanding of God and history: 'In the heart of the night of terror . . . a night of Hiddenness . . . of Doubts and Apostasy . . . came a knock on the door, the knock of the beloved . . . Seven great reversals in Jewish life, seven miracles, commenced – political, military, cultural, theological, life-value, citizenship, and the new fertility of the land of Israel.'

To a surprising degree the answers given by the Holocaust theologians are *the same answers* as those to be found in earlier traditional sources; most are variations on the theme of redemption through suffering, worked out with insights arising from modern psychological and sociological perspectives and applied, often with great sensitivity, to the present situation of the Jewish people. Even those responses, such as that of Rubenstein, which demand radical revision of the traditional concept of God, follow an older theological trend sparked off in reaction to Nietzsche.

God

Why do Jews read Psalm 48, celebrating God's deliverance of Jerusalem from the Assyrian invasion, on Mondays? Israel Lipschütz (1782–1860), famous for his *Commentary* on the Mishna and for frequently fasting three days in succession, suggested that it follows the Sunday Psalm of Creation (Psalm 24) to indicate that God did not 'retire into the firmament and ignore His children' after creation, but bent heaven down to reveal His presence at Sinai.

Packed into this remark are two sharp criticisms. He is rejecting the approach of much of Jewish (as well as Christian and Muslim) medieval philosophy of religion, where God functions as the abstract First Cause or Source of Being, infinitely beyond our powers of comprehension. He is also rejecting a philosophy, Deism, highly popular in the eighteenth century, which admitted the existence of God but regarded him as infinitely remote, unconcerned with the events of our daily lives, and indifferent to the dogma over which religions quarrel. Lipschütz's God is approachable (if demanding), and cares so deeply how 'His children' conduct their lives that He has condescended to reveal the best way to them.

Lipschütz recaptures the God of the Bible and rabbinic tradition, a 'living' God, deeply involved in interaction with humankind. Most subsequent Jewish thinkers have taken this line, ignoring the abstractions and definitions and proofs of existence advanced by the medieval philosophers.

But once you speak of a God who cares, and who interacts, you start to give Him a character. For Reform thinkers such as Hermann Cohen (see p. 102) and Leo Baeck, or a 'modern Orthodox' rabbi such as Samson Raphael Hirsch, God is the God of ethics; they interpret the Torah – even, in Hirsch's case, the most abstruse details of the sacrificial system – as being primarily concerned with ethical values, and hence Israel's mission as to proclaim ethics in the world.

Martin Buber and Emanuel Lévinas put their faith in the God of relationships. *Alles Leben ist Begegnung* ('all life is encounter'), declared Buber, and the important thing is to get your relationship with God and with people right (I–Thou, rather than I–It); from that relationship, which is the essence of Revelation, ethical action flows; laws and rules are feeble attempts to capture revelation, and doomed to inadequacy.

And there are yet more Gods. There is the non-supernatural God whose existence is expressed in the evolving civilization of Judaism (M. M. Kaplan); the transcendent God of *Halakha*, whose supreme revelation is through a perfect, a priori system of law, that confronts and heals the division between the world of science and the world of religion (J. D. Soloveitchik); the 'anthropopathic' God who empathizes with our feelings, shares our hopes and joys and distress and suffering (A. J. Heschel); the God of the Covenant, whose ethical and religious demands are known through his covenental relationship with a community (Borowitz, Novak, Hartman); the God who failed to intervene to rescue the victims of the Holocaust, yet in whose silence and apparent impotence we discover our inmost spirituality (Rubenstein, Kushner); there is even 'the abusing God' (David Blumenthal), with whom we must seek reconciliation as with a parent at whose hand we have suffered.

Whichever it is, God is very much there, alive, interacting. She is not dead. Which brings us to the next point.

Feminism

Economic and social changes in the wake of the Enlightenment and the Industrial Revolution spawned the women's rights movement, also known as feminism or women's liberation, in late eighteenth-century

Europe; women's republican clubs in Revolutionary France pleaded that 'liberty, equality, and fraternity' should apply to all, regardless of sex.

Scientific studies have suggested that many alleged differences between men and women are cultural artefacts rather than physiologically determined characteristics. Language itself, by using the male gender for collective forms, is seen to perpetuate the 'invisibility' or 'otherness' of women, and subordinate them to men. Women's groups have urged the sharing by men of domestic roles, legalization of abortion, and the recognition of lesbian rights. How has all this impacted on Judaism?

The Bible, the Talmud, and pre-modern Judaism take for granted a patriarchal, authoritarian model for society. The creation story of Genesis 2–3, with an Eve moulded from Adam's rib and yielding to temptation, shows the loss of the ideal and justifies the placing of Eve under Adam's authority. Women are prominent or influential either in some 'feminine' capacity (the matriarchs, and Miriam, Ruth, Esther) or as exceptional individuals, whether good (Deborah the Judge, Huldah the prophetess) or bad (Queen Athaliah). God is overwhelmingly male.

But Genesis 1: 27 states clearly enough: 'So God created humankind in his own image; in the image of God he created him; male and female he created them.' This implies that in using our concept of God to model human behaviour we should not distinguish between male and female. Consistent with this, the rabbinic formulation of the 'imitation of God' incorporates virtues associated with female as well as male roles: 'How can a person walk after God? Is it not written "For the Lord your God is a consuming fire"? But follow God's attributes. As He clothes the naked . . . as He visits the sick . . . comforts the bereaved . . . buries the dead . . . so should you.' Distinctively male characteristics are indeed absent from the list. It is God's care and compassion that we are exhorted to copy, not his vengeance and imposition of justice.

If the availability of feminine imagery of God within Jewish tradition is limited, does it make sense to create new images? Rita M. Gross has urged that familiar forms of addressing God in prayer should be transposed to the feminine. For instance *ha-qedosha berukha hi* – 'the Holy One, blessed be She' – should be used in place of the current masculine form. She lists five basic goddess images that need translating into Jewish terms:

- the 'coincidence of opposites' or 'ambiguity symbolism'
- images of God the Mother, which must be joined with
- the goddess of motherhood and culture, twin aspects of creativity
- goddess as giver of wisdom and patron of scholarship and learning
- the assertion of sexuality as an aspect of divinity.

She sums up:

> Dimensions of deity that have been lost or severely attenuated during the long centuries when we spoke of God as if S/He were only a male are restored. They seem to have to do with acceptance of immanence, with nature and the cyclic round. Metaphors of enclosure, inner spaces, and curved lines seem to predominate. What a relief from the partial truth of intervention and transcendence; of history and linear time; of going forth, exposure and straight lines!

Reconstructionist Judaism has had full equality for women since it began in 1968, and has gone further than any other denomination in formulating worship in non-sexist forms. Reform has gradually achieved equality, and many Reform congregations have attempted the required liturgical reform; for instance, the prayer 'God of our fathers, Abraham, Isaac and Jacob' has become 'God of our ancestors: of Abraham, Isaac, and Jacob; of Sarah, Rebekah, Rachel, and Leah'. Conservative Judaism has struggled to achieve equality whilst retaining fidelity to *halakha*; its decision in 1983 to ordain women rabbis caused a split in the movement.

Orthodoxy retains segregated seating in the synagogue, does not call women to the Torah or count them in the prayer quorum let alone ordain them as rabbis, and retains other aspects of traditional *halakha* which appear to denigrate women. Yet even the Orthodox have not remained unaffected by the women's movement; they have improved women's educational facilities and allowed and even encouraged women to take part in public affairs where this is not seen as incompatible with *halakha*. Of note are the Beis Yaakov movement, originating in Poland early in the century to develop girls' education, and the more recent *Rosh Hodesh* (New Moon) movement which has encouraged women's prayer groups and educational activities and, along with other groups, taken vigorous action to secure the acknowledgement of women's rights in the Orthodox community.

Chapter 9
'Eternal law', changing times

We've almost made it. For our final chapter let's take a quick, alphabetic look at some examples of how *poskim* (rabbis who decide the law) have drawn on traditional sources to tackle contemporary problems. This is a crucial exercise. If the Torah is indeed an 'eternal law' as believers claim, it must be possible to obtain guidance from it at all times and in all places. General moral principles are easy enough to derive from the Bible and Talmud, but they don't easily yield clear answers to specific questions.

In Judaism, you find specific answers to your questions through *halakha*, 'law', the process of legal reasoning based on sources and precedents.

Modern advances in the biological sciences and medical technology have generated economic, legal, and ethical questions, few of which were contemplated when the sources of Jewish law were formulated. Our illustrations will all be drawn from this challenging field, in which many thousands of rabbinic *Responsa* (Questions and Answers) have now been published. Hospitals such as Shaare Zedek in Jerusalem have allowed the *halakhic* rulings to be put to the test; academic institutions such as Ben Gurion University in Beer Sheva have chairs in Jewish Medical Ethics; rabbinic organizations such as the Rabbinical Council of America issue regular updates on medical *halakha*; and books and articles on the ethics and *halakha* of medicine are authored by experts from all Jewish denominations.

Conservative and Orthodox rabbis claim to base their decisions on *halakha*, Conservatives laying more stress on historical context.

Not everyone is convinced that the *halakhic* process is sound. Daniel H. Gordis has suggested that the real objections of the Orthodox to artificial insemination by donor (AID) arise not from a genuine *halakhic* argument but from revulsion at the notion of a married woman being impregnated by another man's sperm; they are concerned, rightly, about issues of sexuality, parenthood, and the nature of marriage. 'But if *these* are the issues underlying our objection to AID' comments Gordis, 'we should say so clearly and discuss those issues on their own merits, rather than obscuring the salient halakhic issue by reference to secondary ones.' He therefore favours using the resources of *halakha* not as a system of rules to be subjected to analysis, but as a stockpile to be scoured for its implicit concepts of humanness, of being made in the divine image; it is these concepts on which we should base our decisions in medical ethics. This is roughly the Reform and Reconstructionist position.

Elliott Dorff, focusing on issues at the end of life, finds both the Orthodox and Reform positions unsatisfactory. The Orthodox are dominated by rules and precedents which they misapply or arbitrarily extrapolate because they do not allow sufficiently for the differences between the times in which the precedents were set and the radically different medical situation of our time; the Reform fail because their appeal to concepts such as 'covenantal responsibility' lacks the discipline of *halakha* and is ultimately indistinguishable from liberal secular ethics. His own preference, which he sees as that of the Conservative movement in general, is for a three-stage approach. First, the Jewish conceptual and legal sources must be studied in their historical contexts. On this basis, one can identify the relevant differences between our own situation and that in which the texts were formulated. Then and only then can one apply the sources to the contemporary issue, using not only purely legal reasoning but 'theological deliberations concerning our nature as human beings created by, and in the image of, God'.

Abortion

Foeticide is forbidden in Jewish law, but it is not regarded as homicide. Since it is not homicide, the possibility arises that if giving birth would threaten the mother's life, foeticide would be preferable to letting nature take its course and thereby risking the mother's life. This basic principle governing abortion was formulated in the Mishna (see pp. 33–4): 'If a woman had difficulty in giving birth, they may cut up the child inside her and bring it out piece by piece, since her life has priority over its life. But if the greater part had already come out (been born) they may not touch (harm) it, for one may not set aside one life for another.'

Prima facie, the woman in childbirth appears to be in the situation of a victim pursued by an aggressor, where the law is that the victim should be saved, even if it is necessary to take the life of the pursuer to achieve this. But the same logic would apply even if 'the greater part had been born', for the baby is as much a 'pursuer' as the foetus. The seventeenth-century Polish rabbi Joshua Falk solved this by saying that a baby in the process of birth is not categorized as a pursuer since this is 'the nature of the world', and therefore the mother's life does not have priority over the baby's; but an unborn foetus is not yet in the full sense of the word a *nefesh* (literally 'soul', used here in the sense of 'human person'), so that, although the foetus may not wantonly be killed, he or she remains a 'pursuer'.

Yair Hayyim Bacharach (1638–1701) ruled that, if it were not for the need to promote high moral standards and discourage promiscuity, it would be permissible for a woman who had conceived a child in adultery to take an abortificant to destroy the 'accursed seed within her'. In the following century Jacob Emden raised the question of whether a woman who had conceived a child in adultery might have an abortion to save her from the 'great distress' even though her life was not in danger. Later authorities have been prepared to consider abortion, particularly where the foetus is less than forty days old, if great distress or shame would be caused to the mother by bringing the pregnancy to full term.

The debate came to a head with a dispute between two of the leading *poskim* of the twentieth century, Moshe Feinstein (1895–1986) and Eliezer Yehuda Waldenburg, as to whether it was permitted to abort a foetus known to have Tay-Sachs disease, a congenital condition involving physical and mental retardation, loss of sight and hearing, and death by the age of 3 or 4. Waldenburg, citing Emden's precedent, permitted abortion even as late as the seventh month, to avoid the 'great distress' to both mother and child from such a tragic birth. Feinstein opposed this, since no direct threat was involved to the mother's life, and abortion, though not technically homicide, is definitely forbidden under normal circumstances as a form of homicide. Feinstein was clearly concerned by the growing tendency in the USA at that time to permit abortion on medical, social, and 'private' grounds; in his evidently strong moral concern he takes a firm stance against the permissiveness of the age.

None of the *halakhic* arguments for or against abortion has to do with the rights of women over their bodies or, for that matter, with the rights of men over their womenfolk. The issue concerns only (*a*) the woman's own right to life, and (*b*) the rights of an embyro or foetus. Where these rights conflict it is necessary to enquire into the strength of the rights of the embryo or foetus; though some rights may be acquired at conception the full range and full force of human rights commences only at birth.

No Jewish authority permits abortion simply as a method of birth control.

Artificial insemination

Halakha faces three problems in considering the permissibility or otherwise of artificial insemination by donor:

1. Is the child of a married women who became pregnant from a man other than her husband, but without a normal act of intercourse, a *mamzer* (illegitimate)? Put another way, is the woman an adulteress?
2. Even if the woman's own husband was the donor, could the insemination take place when she is still *niddah* (technically in a state of menstruation, not having bathed in a *mikveh* since her last period)?
3. Since masturbation is in other circumstances forbidden, how should sperm be obtained from the husband or donor?

Although artificial insemination appears to be a novel problem of the twentieth century, precedent was found in a Talmudic reference to the possibility of a virgin who had conceived 'in a bath place' – that is, by accidentally absorbing sperm deposited there. The case was much discussed in the Middle Ages; Simon ben Zemah Duran (1361–1444) reports that 'a number of non-Jews' as well as another rabbi had told him of virgins they knew of who had become pregnant in this manner. Simon may have been unduly credulous, but even if the incidents were purely imaginary the legal precedents were set.

Rabbi Moshe Feinstein argued that, where there was no forbidden sexual act, no adultery could be deemed to have taken place and therefore a child conceived in such a way would not be a *mamzer*. Whilst not positively encouraging anyone to practise artificial insemination, he argued that it was not actually forbidden.

Feinstein was bitterly attacked for his permissiveness by Rabbi Jacob Breisch, who castigated artificial insemination by a donor as abominable, forbidden, and disgusting, whilst conceding that the child could not be considered a *mamzer* nor its mother an adulteress, and that artificial insemination by the husband might be permitted. Breisch's opposition seems to have been based more on a sort of Jewish public-relations concern than on a specific *halakha* to do with insemination; he felt that Jews should not appear more permissive in moral issues than Christians, and, as the Catholic Church had condemned artificial insemination, it would degrade Judaism if Jews were to be more lax. Feinstein rejected this argument out of hand, possibly reflecting a difference between American and European attitudes.

Joel Teitelbaum, the Hasidic rabbi of Satmar, and Feinstein's sharpest opponent, took the position that adultery was constituted by the deposition, by whatever means, of a man's sperm in a woman married to someone else. Feinstein had no difficulty in demonstrating the absence of *halakhic* support for such a position.

Euthanasia

Three types of 'mercy killing' may be considered. Eugenic euthanasia – that is, the killing of handicapped or 'socially undesirable' individuals – is in no way countenanced in Judaism. Debate centres on (*a*) active euthanasia, where a drug or other treatment is administered to hasten the patient's release from suffering, or (*b*) passive euthanasia, where therapy is withheld and the patient is allowed to die naturally.

An early rabbinic source unequivocally states that 'One who is dying is regarded as a living person in all respects . . . one may not bind his jaws, stop up his openings . . . Move him . . . One may not close the eyes of the dying person. If anyone touches or moves them it is as if he shed blood, as Rabbi Meir said, "This is like a flickering flame; as soon as anyone touches it, it goes out." Likewise, if anyone closes the eyes of the dying it is as if he had taken his life.' The main Codes rule that if something – for instance, the noise of chopping wood – is preventing 'the soul from departing', one may cease the activity in order to ease death.

These two rulings establish the distinction between active and passive euthanasia, and much subsequent *halakha* hinges on refining and applying the distinction to contemporary situations. Active euthanasia is generally regarded as murder; passive euthanasia may sometimes be permitted. Physicians are urged to do their utmost to save and prolong life, even for a short time, and even if the patient is suffering great distress. Some authorities maintain that withdrawal of life-support is unlike 'removing the noise of chopping wood' referred to in the classical sources; life-support is positive therapy, whereas extraneous noise is simply an obstacle to death. Others are not so sure of the distinction.

Waldenburg permitted the use of narcotics and analgesics to relieve the pain of the dying even though these drugs might depress the activity of the respiratory system and hasten death, provided the intention of administering the drugs was solely to relieve pain. Moreover, one may not initiate artificial life-support for a patient who is incurably and irreversibly ill, though, where artificial life-support apparatus has been connected, it may not be disconnected until the patient is dead according to the criteria of *halakha*. To evade the harshness of the latter ruling, Waldenburg made the novel suggestion that respirators be set with automatic time clocks; since they would disconnect automatically after the set period, a positive decision would be required to continue their operation, and this would not be done unless there was now hope of cure.

The twelfth-century Tosafist Jacob Tam seems to imply that it is permitted actively to take one's own life to avoid excessive torture, though it is unclear whether he meant this only in those circumstances where the suicide is primarily intended to save the individual from worse sin. Byron L. Sherwin has cited this and similar rulings as a basis for reconsidering the case for active euthanasia; such arguments have made little headway amongst the Orthodox, though Conservative and Reform Jews have been more amenable.

Even though one may not take active, or in many cases even passive, measures to hasten the death of one who is suffering, many halakhists argue that it is permissible to pray for his or her release; the Talmud itself records, apparently with approval, that the maidservant of Judah Ha-Nasi (see p. 32), when she saw his agony, prayed 'Those above [i.e. the angels] seek the master, and those below [i.e. the friends and disciples of Judah] seek him; may those above overcome those below.' The nineteenth-century Turkish rabbi Hayyim Palaggi observed that this should be done only by persons who are not related to the sufferer; relatives might be improperly motivated.

Surrogate motherhood

In Jewish law both maternity and paternity are tied to the 'natural' parent, and this cannot be changed by a court even by a process of adoption. If a woman gives birth to a baby from an implanted ovary, an implanted egg, or a foetal transplant, the baby is not genetically hers. So far as respect of parents is concerned, even an adoptive parent must be respected. But how does the hiatus between genetic and gestational motherhood affect inheritance, incest, and redemption of the first born?

The present Orthodox consensus appears to be that if conception and implantation occurred in a woman's body, the child is hers even if the foetus was subsequently transplanted; some hold that this applies only if the transfer took place more than forty days after conception, since until forty days after conception the foetus was 'mere water'. If conception occurred *in vitro*, the mother is the woman in whom the embryo was implanted and who gave birth to the child. Children conceived by a woman who had received an ovarian transplant are hers.

Evidently, the Orthodox have decided to ignore genetic considerations; at least, their position accords with the sources, which are of course ignorant of genetics. The Talmudic understanding of the roles of the sexes in reproduction was not that father and mother contributed complementary sets of genes but rather that the father provided the 'seed' and the mother the 'soil' in which the child was nurtured. Thus J. David Bleich is in error when he concludes from analysis of a Talmudic passage that 'Maternal identity is established in the first instance by production of the gamete'; the gamete, and even the ovum, are unknown in the traditional sources of *halakha*.

Conclusion

Similar illustrations could be drawn from almost every field of contemporary life, as *poskim* seek guidance from Bible, Talmud, and rabbinic tradition in such manners as the status of women, the conduct of warfare, the ethics of commerce, the protection of the environment, and all aspects of human relationships and religious ritual. In each of these fields the different approaches to use of sources by Orthodox, Conservative, and Reform reappear.

Add to this programme of decision-making the philosophical and theological speculation by which traditional teaching is rendered intelligible in the modern world, the soul-searching demanded in the aftermath of the Shoah, and the challenge of the novel experience for Jews of political empowerment. Never – certainly not since the days of Late Antiquity – has the Jewish world experienced such intellectual and emotional turbulence.

Yet never has it produced such vigorous responses. Our brief look at Judaism has indicated something of the wealth and variety of these responses, which give testimony to the ongoing vitality of an ancient tradition always ready to renew itself in a changing world.

The way ahead will not be easy. Peace remains elusive in the Land of Israel, diaspora Jewry suffers from assimilation and diminishing numbers, and religious and political divisions persist. Yet only the mean of spirit will fail to discern within the turmoil a sense of rediscovery and renewal which bode well for the future of a historic faith and people.

Appendix A
The Thirteen Principles of the Faith

First formulated by Moses Maimonides in his *Commentary on the Mishna* composed c.1160.

I believe with perfect faith that:

1. The Creator is Author and Guide of everything that exists.
2. The Creator is One; His unity is unlike that of anything else; He is our God and exists eternally.
3. The Creator has no body or physical characteristics, and cannot be compared with anything that exists.
4. The Creator is first and last of all beings.
5. It is right to pray to the Creator, but to no other being.
6. All the words of the prophets are true.
7. The prophecy of Moses is true, and He was the father (that is, the greatest) of all prophets, both before and after Him.
8. The Torah now in our possession is that given to Moses.
9. TheTorahwillnotbechanged,norwilltheCreatorgiveanyotherTorah.
10. The Creator knows the deeds and thoughts of people.
11. He rewards those who keep His commandments, and punishes those who disobey.
12. Though the Messiah delay, one must constantly expect His coming.
13. The dead will be resurrected.

Appendix B
The 'Philadelphia Platform' of Reform Judaism

The Philadelphia Conference, 3–6 November, 1869.

Statement of Principles

1. The Messianic aim of Israel is not the restoration of the old Jewish state under a descendant of David, involving a second separation from the nations of the earth, but the union of all the children of God in the confession of the unity of God, so as to realize the unity of all rational creatures and their call to moral sanctification.

2. We look upon the destruction of the second Jewish commonwealth not as a punishment for the sinfulness of Israel, but as a result of the divine purpose revealed to Abraham, which, as has become ever clearer in the course of the world's history, consists in the dispersion of the Jews to all parts of the earth, for the realization of their high-priestly mission, to lead the nations to the true knowledge and worship of God.

3. The Aaronic priesthood and the Mosaic sacrificial cult were preparatory steps to the real priesthood of the whole people, which began with the dispersion of the Jews, and to the sacrifices of sincere devotion and moral sanctification, which alone are pleasing and acceptable to the Most Holy. These institutions, preparatory to higher religiosity, were consigned to the past, once for all, with the destruction of the Second Temple, and only in this

sense – as educational influences in the past – are they to be mentioned in our prayers.

4. Every distinction between Aaronides and non-Aaronides, as far as religious rites and duties are concerned, is consequently inadmissible, both in the religious cult and in social life.

5. The selection of Israel as the people of religion, as the bearer of the highest idea of humanity, is still, as ever, to be strongly emphasized, and for this very reason, whenever this is mentioned, it shall be done with full emphasis laid on the world-embracing mission of Israel and the love of God for all His children.

6. The belief in the bodily resurrection has no religious foundation, and the doctrine of immortality refers to the after-existence of the soul only.

7. Urgently as the cultivation of the Hebrew language, in which the treasures of the divine revelation were given and the immortal remains of a literature that influences all civilized nations are preserved, must always be desired by us in fulfilment of a sacred duty, yet it has become unintelligible to the vast majority of our coreligionists; therefore, as is advisable under existing circumstances, it must give way in prayer to intelligible language, which prayer, if not understood, is a soulless form.

The conference also passed resolutions on marriage and divorce, and whilst accepting the matrilineal principle for determining Jewish status, emphasized that the child of a Jewish mother was Jewish even if an uncircumcised male.

Suggestions for Further Reading

One of the easiest ways to find out more about Judaism is to browse through the pages of the 20 volume English language *Encyclopedia Judaica*, published in Jerusalem in 1972. There are also numerous single volume dictionaries and enclopaedias available, including a one-volume edition of the *Judaica*.

Try to meet Jews and talk to them, read the Jewish Press, absorb what you can through the novels and stories of writers such as Isaac Bashevis Singer, Chaim Potok, and Elie Wiesel. Videos and CDs with Jewish content abound, and the Internet has innumerable sites with an interest in Jews, Judaism, or Israel.

A word of warning, though. Translations are available of classics of rabbinic Judaism including the Talmud. But if you really want to delve into the primary sources, even in translation, you will need a teacher. It is not that the texts are deliberately obscure, but rather that the whole way of thinking relates to a civilization very different from our own, and you need an expert to 'unpack' the meaning for you.

The following chapter by chapter suggestions are for those who want to follow up ideas in this book:

Introduction

Klenicki, Leon, and Wigoder, Geoffrey, *A Dictionary of the Jewish–Christian Dialogue* (New York: Paulist Press, 1984).

Kochan, Lionel, *The Jew and his History* (New York: Schocken Books, 1977).

Chapter 1

Lewis, Bernard, *The Jews of Islam* (Princeton NJ: Princeton University Press, 1984).

Meyer, Michael A., *Jewish Identity in the Modern World* (Seattle & London: University of Washington Press, 1990).

Webber, Jonathan (ed.), *Jewish Identities in the New Europe* (London and Washington: Oxford Centre for Hebrew and Jewish Studies with the Littman Library of Jewish Civilization, 1994).

Chapter 2

Shanks, Hershel (ed.), *Christianity and Rabbinic Judaism: A Parallel History of Their Origins and Early Development* (Washington: Biblical Archaeology Society, 1992).

Neusner, Jacob, *Vanquished Nation, Broken Spirit: The Virtues of the Heart in Formative Judaism* (Cambridge, London, etc.: Cambridge University Press, 1987).

Saperstein, Marc, *Moments of Crisis in Jewish-Christian Relations* (London/Philadelphia: SCM Press/Trinity Press International, 1989).

De Lange, Nicholas, *Origen and the Jews* (Cambridge: Cambridge University Press, 1976).

Chapter 3

Urbach, Ephraim E., tr. I. Abrahams, *The Sages* (Cambridge, MA and London: Harvard University Press, 1987).

Saadia, Gaon, tr. Samuel Rosenblatt, *The Book of Beliefs and Opinions* (New Haven: Yale University Press and London: Oxford University Press, 1948).

Twersky, I. (ed.), *A Maimonides Reader* (New York: Behrman House, 1972).

Sorkin, David, *Moses Mendelssohn and the Religious Enlightenment* (London: Peter Halban, 1996).

Chapter 4

Agnon, S. Y., *Days of Awe* (New York: Schocken Books, 1965).

Greenberg, Irving, *The Jewish Way: Living the Holidays* (New York, London: Summit Books, 1988).

The Jewish Catalog, complied and edited by Richard Siegel and others. (Philadelphia; Jewish Publication Society of America.) The first *Catalog* is undated, the second is 1976. These *Catalogs* and their successors are lively 'do-it-yourself kits' of resources for practical Judaism.

Chapter 5

The Daily Prayer Book of the United Hebrew Congregations of the British Commonwealth of Nations (Centenary Edition; London: Singer's Prayer Book Publication Committee, 1990).

Siddur Lev Chadash (Prayer Book) (Union of Liberal and Progressive Synagogues, London 1995/5755).

Green, Arthur S. (ed.), *Jewish Spirituality* (2 vols.) (New York: Routledge & Kegan Paul and London: SCM, 1987).

Jacobs, Louis, *Hasidic Prayer; With a new introduction* (London and Washington: Littman Library of Jewish Civilization, 1993 (2nd edition)).

Umansky, Ellen, and Ashton, Dianne, *Four Centuries of Jewish Women's Spirituality: A Sourcebook* (Boston: Beacon Press, 1992).

Chapter 6

Geffen, Rela M. (ed.), *Celebration and Renewal: Rites of Passage in Judaism* (Philadelphia and Jerusalem: Jewish Publication Society, 1993).

Chapter 7

Meyer, Michael A., *Response to Modernity: A History of the Reform*

Movement in Judaism (New York, Oxford: Oxford University Press, 1988).

The Jew in the Modern World: A Documentary History, Paul Mendes-Flohr and Yehuda Reinharz (eds.) (New York and Oxford: Oxford University Press, 1980).

Alpert, Rebecca T., and Staub, Jacob J., *Exploring Judaism: A Reconstructionist Approach* (New York: Reconstructionist Press, 1985).

Raphael, M. L., *Profiles in American Judaism: The Reform, Conservative, Orthodox and Reconstructionist Traditions in Historical Perspective* (San Francisco: 1984).

Bulka, R. (ed.), *Dimensions of Orthodox Judaism* (New York: 1983).

Chapter 8

Vital, David, *The Origins of Zionism* (Oxford: Clarendon Press, 1975).

Marrus, Michael, *The Holocaust in History* (Penguin Books, 1987).

Blumenthal, David J., *Facing the Abusing* God (Louisville KY: Westminster/John Knox, 1993).

Plaskow, Judith, *Standing Again at Sinai: Judaism from a Feminist Perspective* (San Francisco: Harper, 1991).

Contemporary Jewish Religious Thought, Arthur Cohen and Paul Mendes-Flohr (eds.) (New York: Free Press, 1987).

Chapter 9

Bleich, J. David, *Bioethical Dilemmas: A Jewish Perspective* (Hoboken NJ: Ktav, 1998).

Feldman, David, *Marital Relations, Birth Control and Abortion in Jewish Law* (New York: Schocken Books, 1974).

Dorff, Elliot N., and Newman, Louis E., *Contemporary Jewish Ethics and Morality: A Reader* (New York, Oxford: Oxford University Press, 1995).

Bleich, J. David, *Contemporary Halakhic Problems* (vol. 3) (New York: Ktav, 1989).

Index

Expand your collection of
VERY SHORT INTRODUCTIONS

Visit the
VERY SHORT INTRODUCTIONS
Web site

www.oup.co.uk/vsi

➤ **Information** about all published titles

➤ News of **forthcoming books**

➤ **Extracts** from the books, including titles not yet published

➤ **Reviews** and views

➤ **Links** to other **web sites** and main OUP web page

➤ Information about **VSIs in translation**

➤ **Contact** the editors

➤ **Order** other **VSIs** on-line

BUDDHISM
A Very Short Introduction
Damien Keown

From its origin in India over two thousand years
ago Buddhism has spread throughout Asia and is now
exerting an increasing influence on western culture. In
clear and straightforward language, and with the help of
maps, diagrams and illustrations, this book explains how
Buddhism began and how it evolved into its present-day
form. The central teachings and practices are set out
clearly, and keys topics such as karma and rebirth, medi-
tation, ethics, and Buddhism in the West receive detailed
coverage in separate chapters. The distinguishing features of the main schools – such as Tibetan and Zen
Buddhism – are clearly explained. The book will be
of interest to anyone seeking a sound basic
understanding of Buddhism.

> 'Damien Keown's book is a readable and wonderfully
> lucid introduction to one of mankind's most beautiful,
> profound, and compelling systems of wisdom. His
> impressive powers of explanation help us to come to
> terms with a vital contemporary reality.'
>
> **Bryan Appleyard**

www.oup.co.uk/vsi/buddhism

ISLAM
A Very Short Introduction
Malise Ruthven

Islam features widely in the news, often in its most militant versions, but few people in the non-Muslim world really understand the nature of Islam.

Malise Ruthven's Very Short Introduction contains essential insights into issues such as why Islam has such major divisions between movements such as the Shi'ites, the Sunnis, and the Wahhabis, and the central importance of the Shar'ia (Islamic law) in Islamic life. It also offers fresh perspectives on contemporary questions: Why is the greatest 'Jihad' (holy war) now against the enimies of Islam, rather than the struggle against evil? Can women find fulfilment in Islamic societies? How must Islam adapt as it confronts the modern world?

'Malise Ruthven's book answers the urgent need for an introduction to Islam. ... He addresses major issues with clarity and directness, engages dispassionately with the disparate stereotypes and polemics on the subject, and guides the reader surely through urgent debates about fundamentalism.'

Michael Gilsenan, New York University

www.oup.co.uk/vsi/islam

THEOLOGY
A Very Short Introduction
David F. Ford

This Very Short Introduction provides both believers and non-believers with a balanced survey of the central questions of contemporary theology. David Ford's interrogative approach draws the reader into considering the principles underlying religious belief, including the centrality of salvation to most major religions, the concept of God in ancient, modern, and post-modern contexts, the challenge posed to theology by prayer and worship, and the issue of sin and evil. He also probes the nature of experience, knowledge, and wisdom in theology, and discusses what is involved in interpreting theological texts today.

> 'David Ford tempts his readers into the huge resources of theology with an attractive mix of simple questions and profound reflection. With its vivid untechnical language it succeeds brilliantly in its task of introduction.'
> **Stephen Sykes, University of Durham**

> 'a fine book, imaginatively conceived and gracefully written. It carries the reader along with it, enlarging horizons while acknowledging problems and providing practical guidance along the way.'
> **Maurice Wiles, University of Oxford**

www.oup.co.uk/vsi/theology